SELFISH PIGS

ANDY RILEY IS THE AUTHOR/ARTIST OF:

THE BOOK OF BUNNY SUICIDES, RETURN OF THE BUNNY SUICIDES, GREAT LIES TO TELL SMALL KIDS, LOADS MORE LIES TO TELL SMALL KIDS, THE BUMPER BOOK OF BUNNY SUICIDES AND D.I.Y. DENTISTRY (AND OTHER ALARMING INVENTIONS). HIS WEEKLY CARTOON STRIP, ROASTED, RUNS IN THE OBSERVER MAGAZINE AND IS ALSO COMPILED AS A HODDER & STOUGHTON HARDBACK.

HIS SCRIPTWRITING WORK INCLUDES BLACK BOOKS, HYPERDRIVE, LITTLE BRITAIN, THE ARMSTRONG AND MILLER SHOW, SMACK THE PONY, THE ARMANDO IANNUCCI SHOWS, SO GRAHAM NORTON, THE 99P CHALLENGE, SLACKER CATS, SPITTING IMAGE, KATY BRAND'S BIG ASS SHOW, THE FRIDAY NIGHT ARMISTICE, AND THE BAFTA-WINNING ANIMATION ROBBIE THE REINDEER.

LOOK OUT FOR NEW CARTOONS AT:
misterandyriley.com

ON TWITTER:
@ andyrileyish

SELFISH PIGS

--ADORABLY AWFUL LITTLE SWINE--

Andy Riley

IT'S MY BOAT

GO AWAY

THREE RIVERS PRESS
NEW YORK

PUBLISHED IN THE UNITED STATES BY THREE RIVERS PRESS, AN IMPRINT OF THE CROWN PUBLISHING GROUP, A DIVISION OF RANDOM HOUSE, INC., NEW YORK. WWW. CROWNPUBLISHING. COM ⌇ THREE RIVERS PRESS AND THE TUGBOAT DESIGN ARE REGISTERED TRADEMARKS OF RANDOM HOUSE, INC. ⌇ ORIGINALLY PUBLISHED IN GREAT BRITAIN BY HODDER & STOUGHTON, A HACHETTE U.K. COMPANY, LONDON, IN 2009.

LIBRARY OF CONGRESS CATALOGING-IN-PUBLICATION DATA:
RILEY, ANDY. SELFISH PIGS: ADORABLY AWFUL LITTLE SWINE / ANDY RILEY.
1. ENGLISH WIT AND HUMOR, PICTORIAL. 2. SWINE - CARICATURES AND CARTOONS. 3. SELFISHNESS - CARICATURES AND CARTOONS. I. TITLE.
NC 1479. R55A4 2010 ⌇ 741.5'6941 — dc 22 ⌇ 2010005956.
ISBN 978-0-307-71844-0 ⌇ PRINTED IN THE UNITED STATES OF AMERICA.

10 9 8 7 6 5 4 3 2 1
FIRST U.S. EDITION

WWW. MISTERANDYRILEY. COM

WITH THANKS TO:

CAMILLA HORNBY, BEN DUNN, JACK FOGG,
GORDON WISE, POLLY FABER, KEVIN CECIL,
KATIE DAVISON, HODDER AND STOUGHTON
AND ALL AT THREE RIVERS PRESS

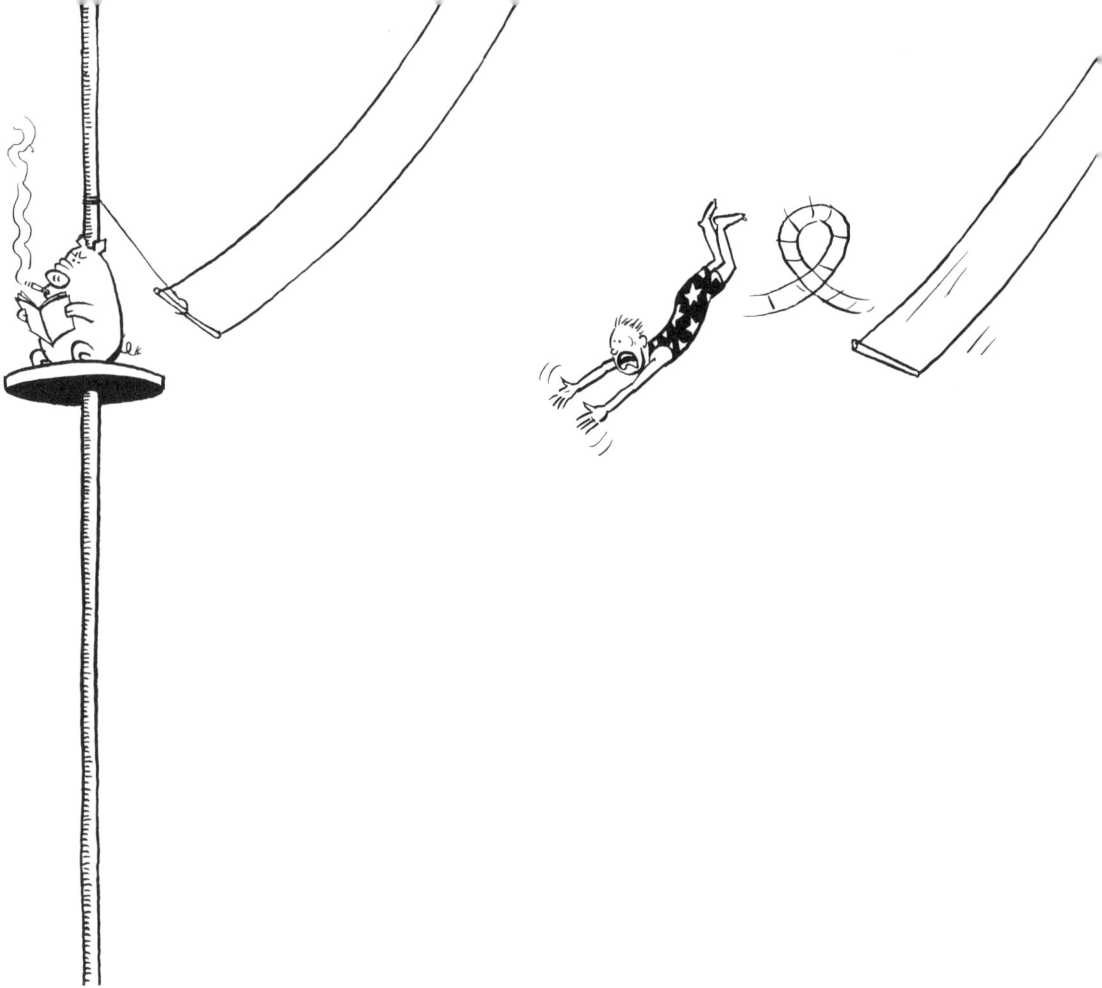

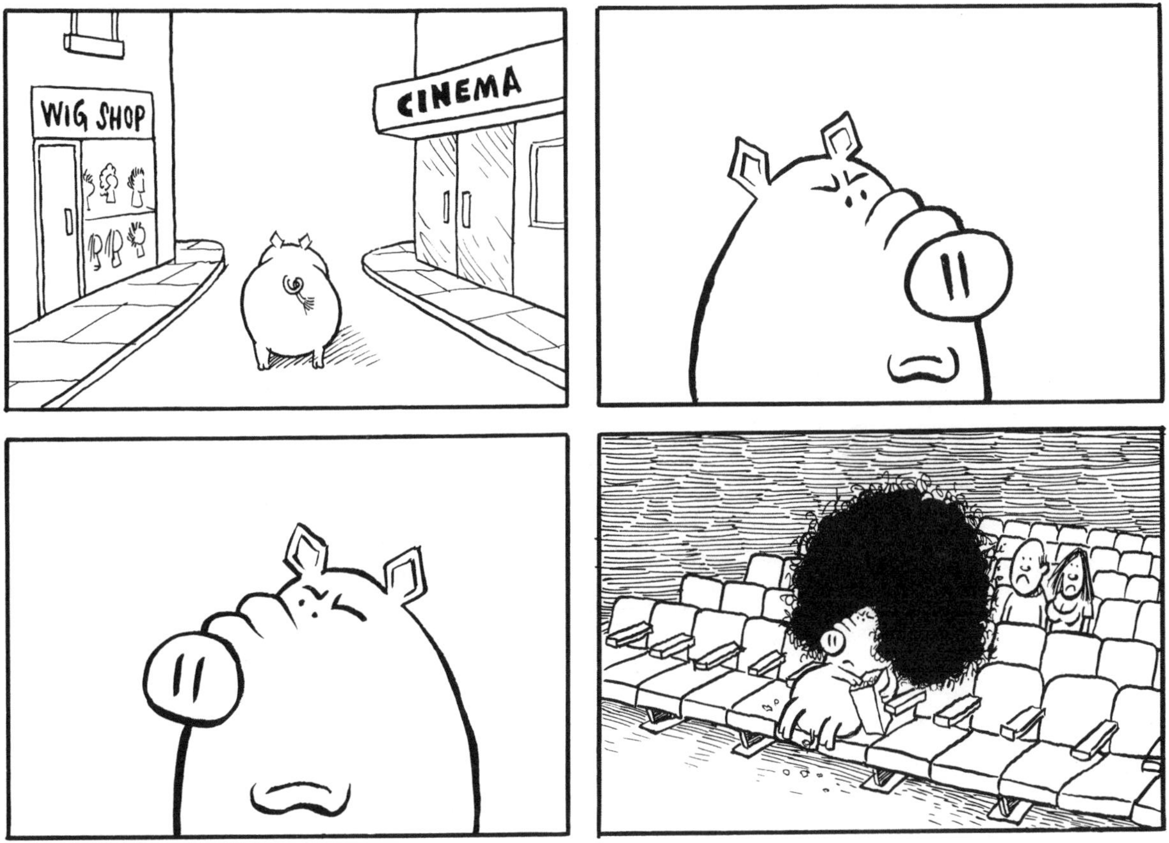
WIG SHOP
CINEMA

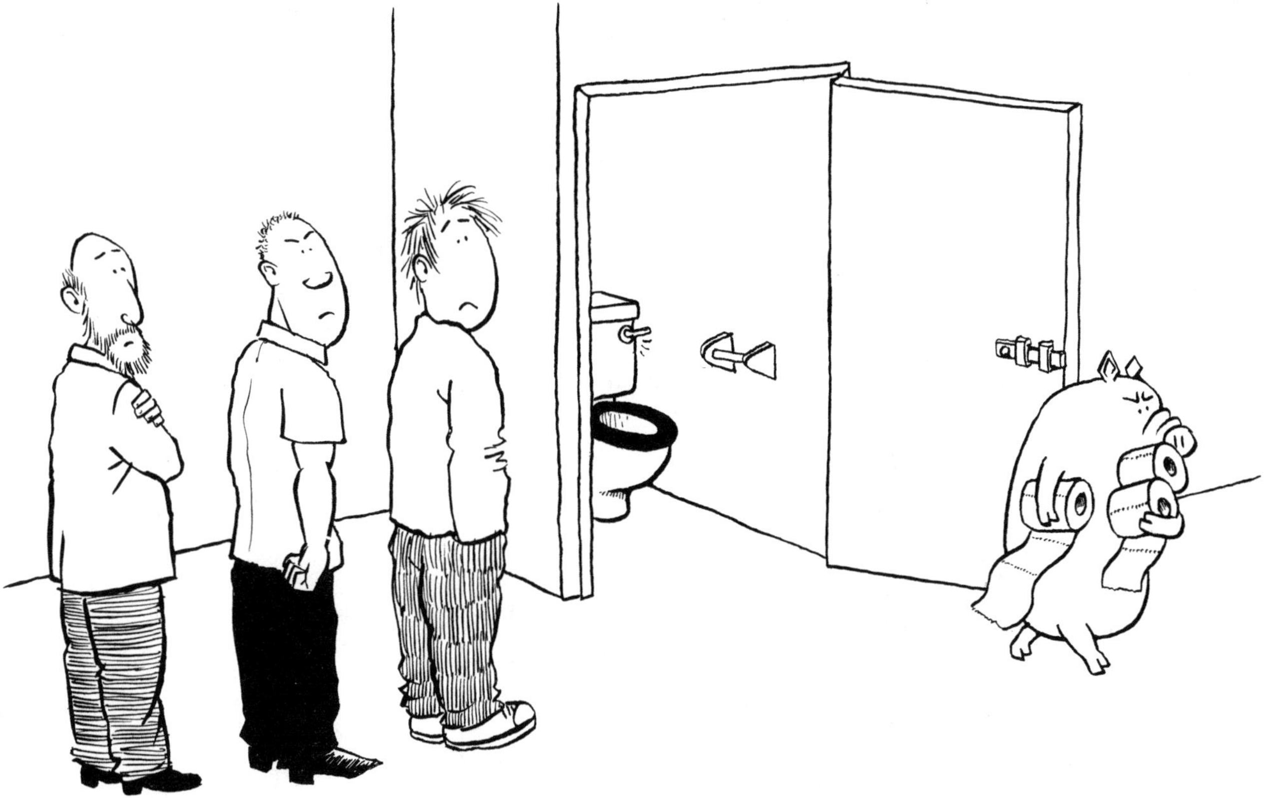

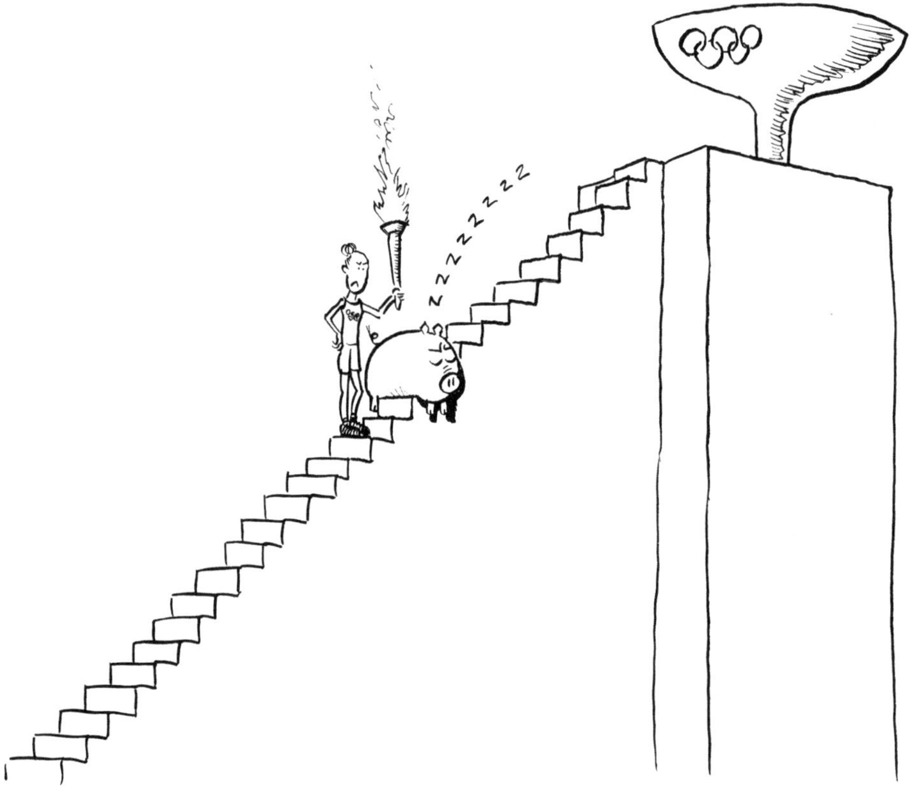
ZZZZZZZZZ

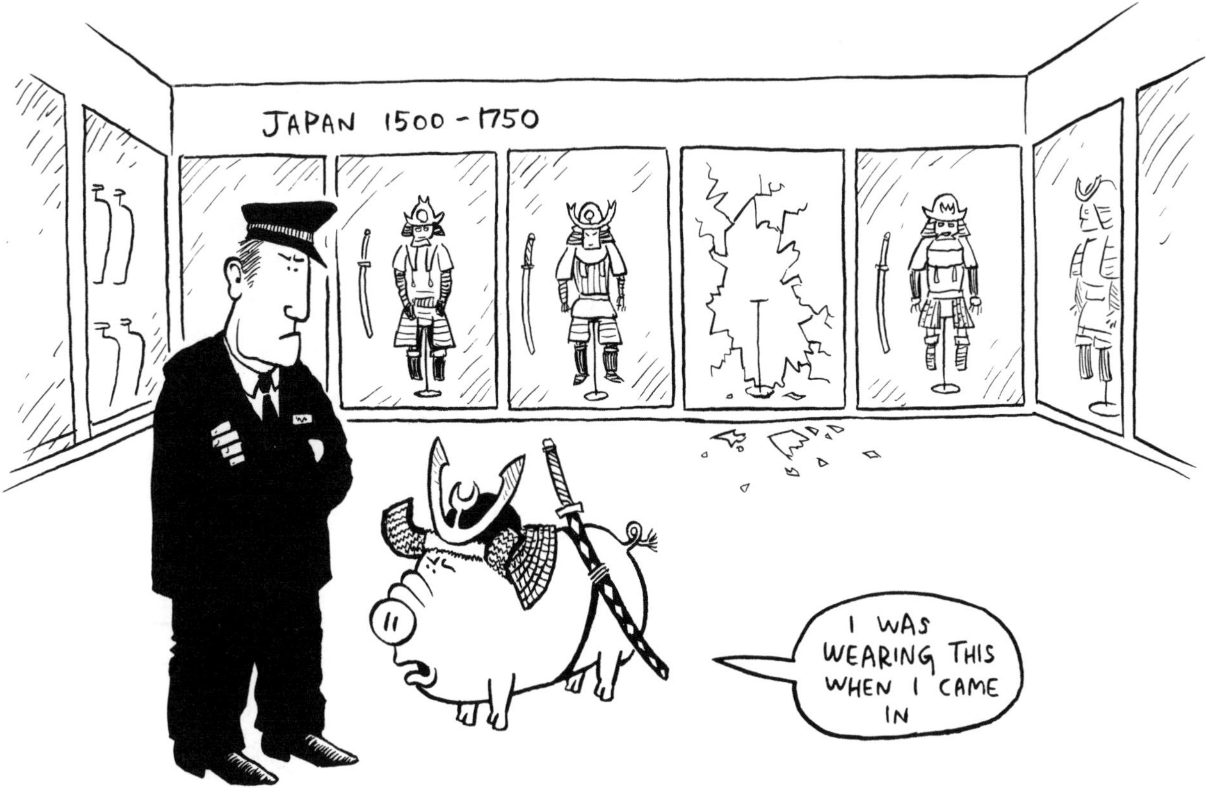
JAPAN 1500 - 1750
I WAS WEARING THIS WHEN I CAME IN

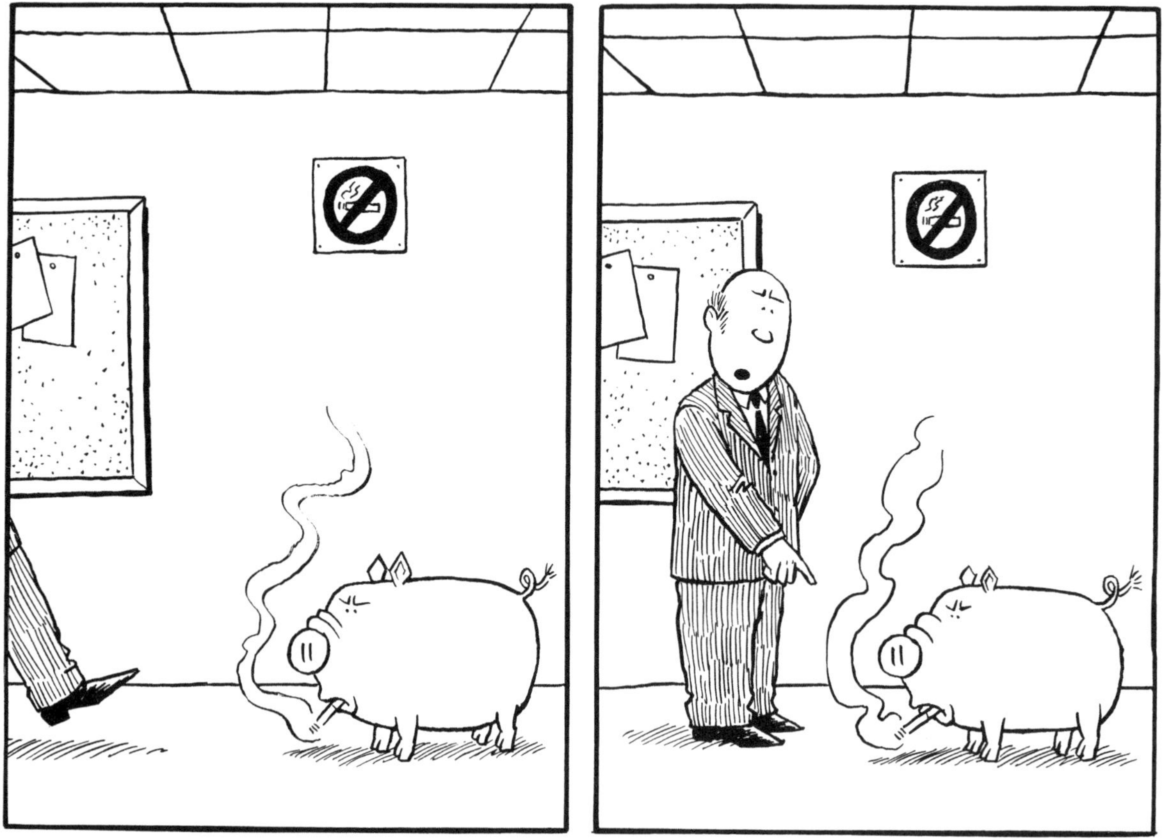

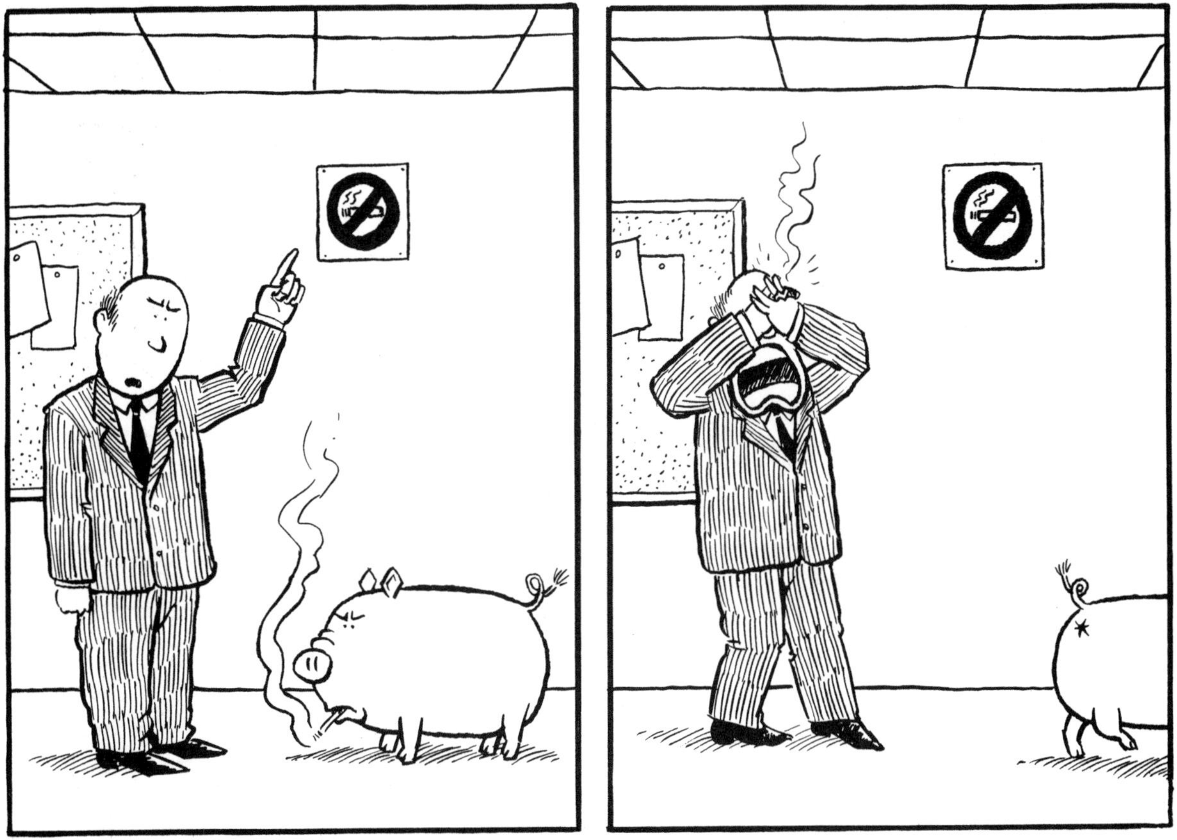

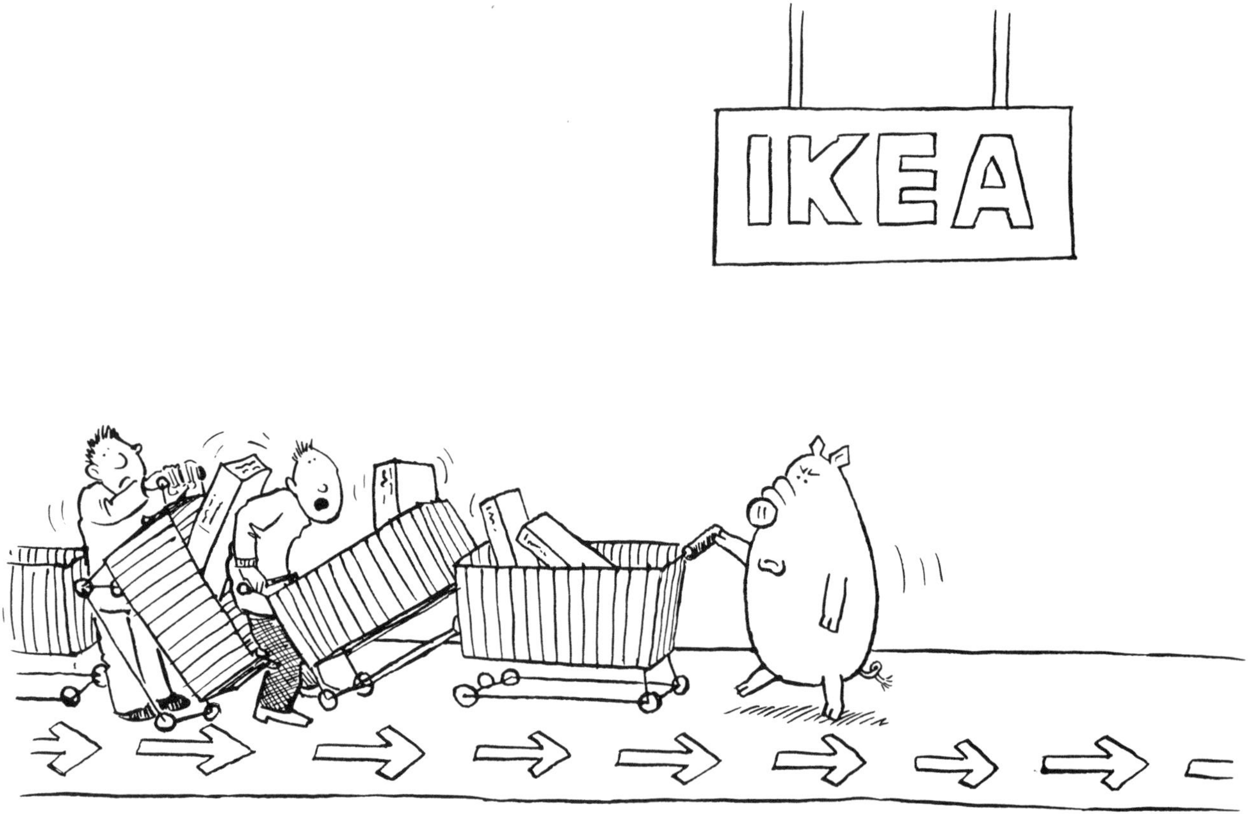
IKEA

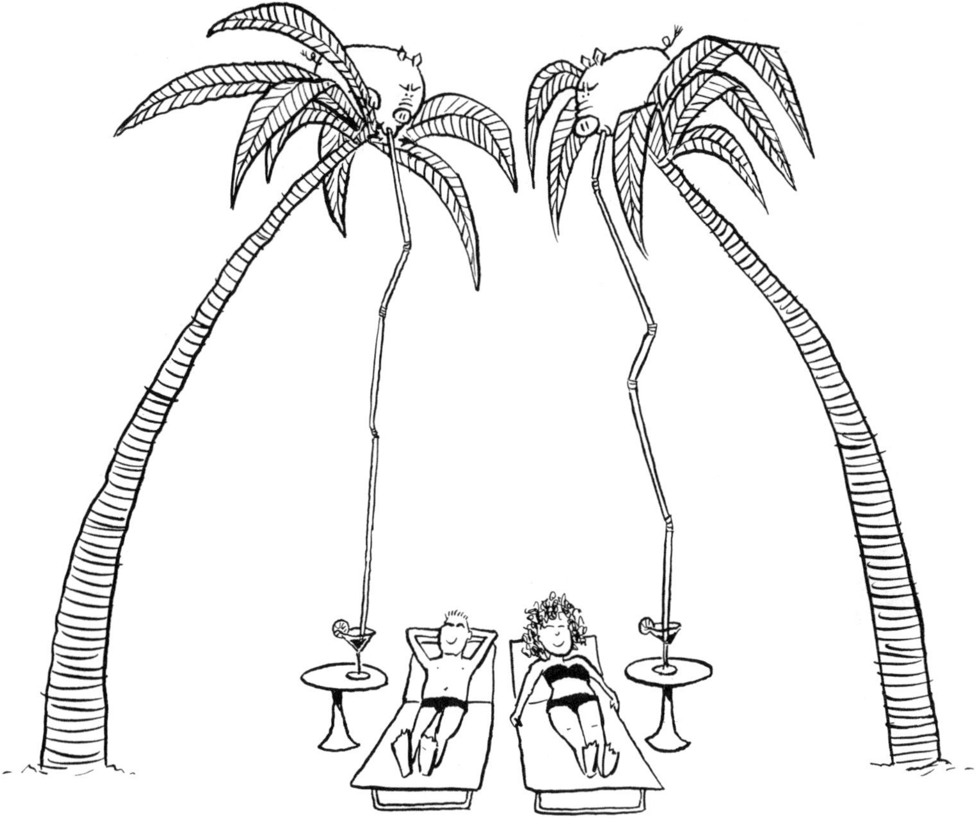

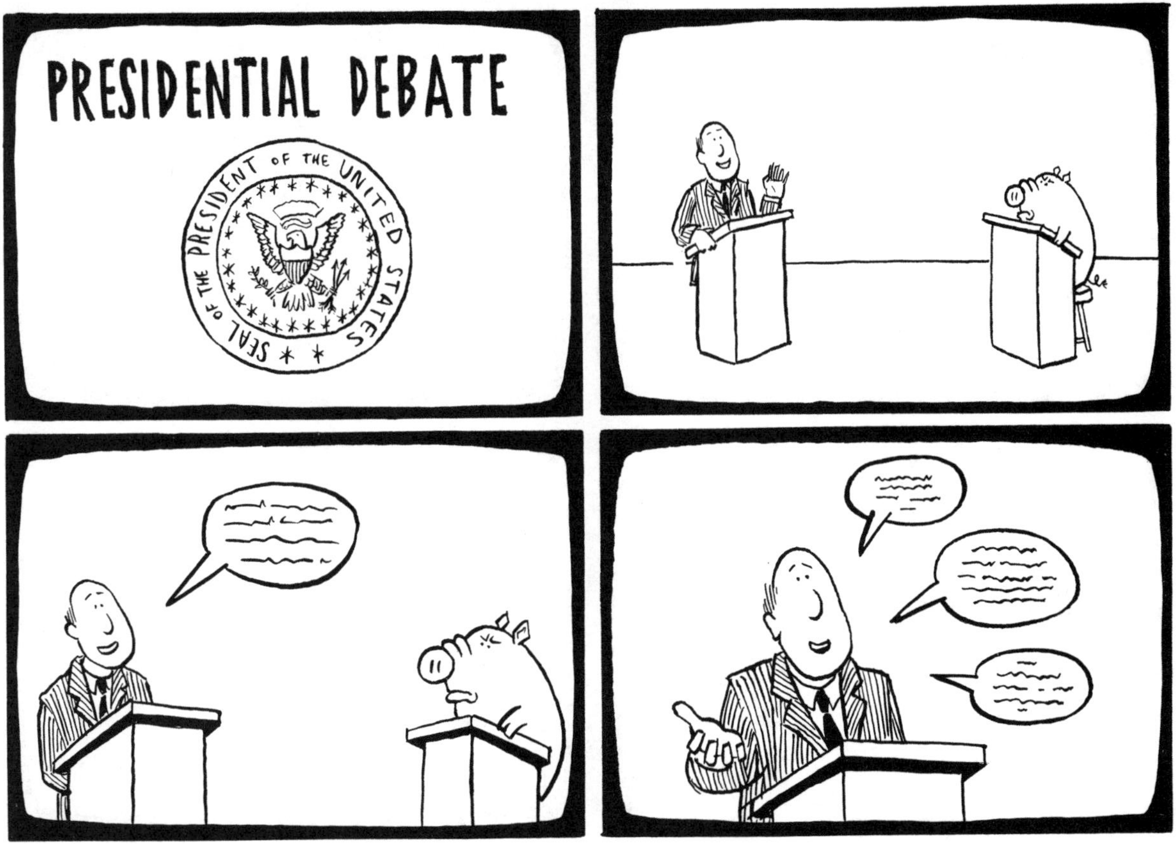
PRESIDENTIAL DEBATE
SEAL OF THE PRESIDENT OF THE UNITED STATES

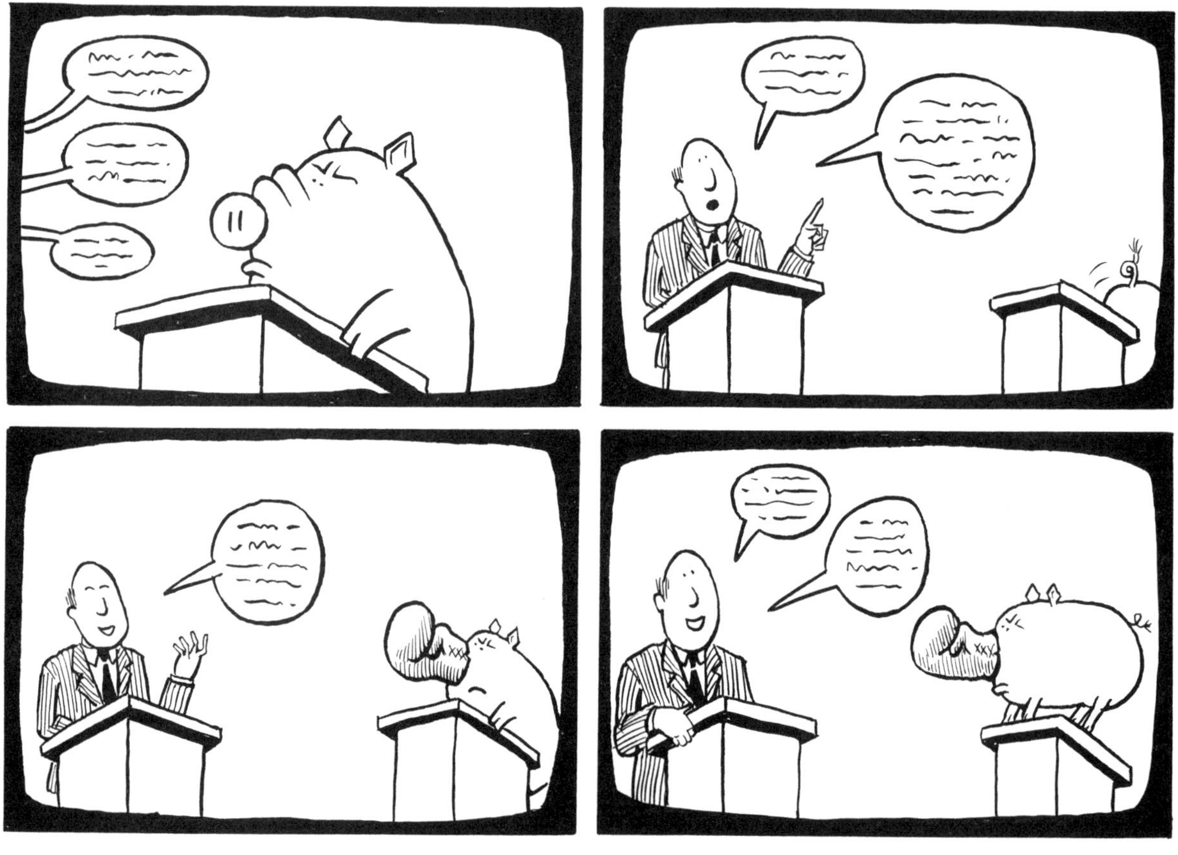

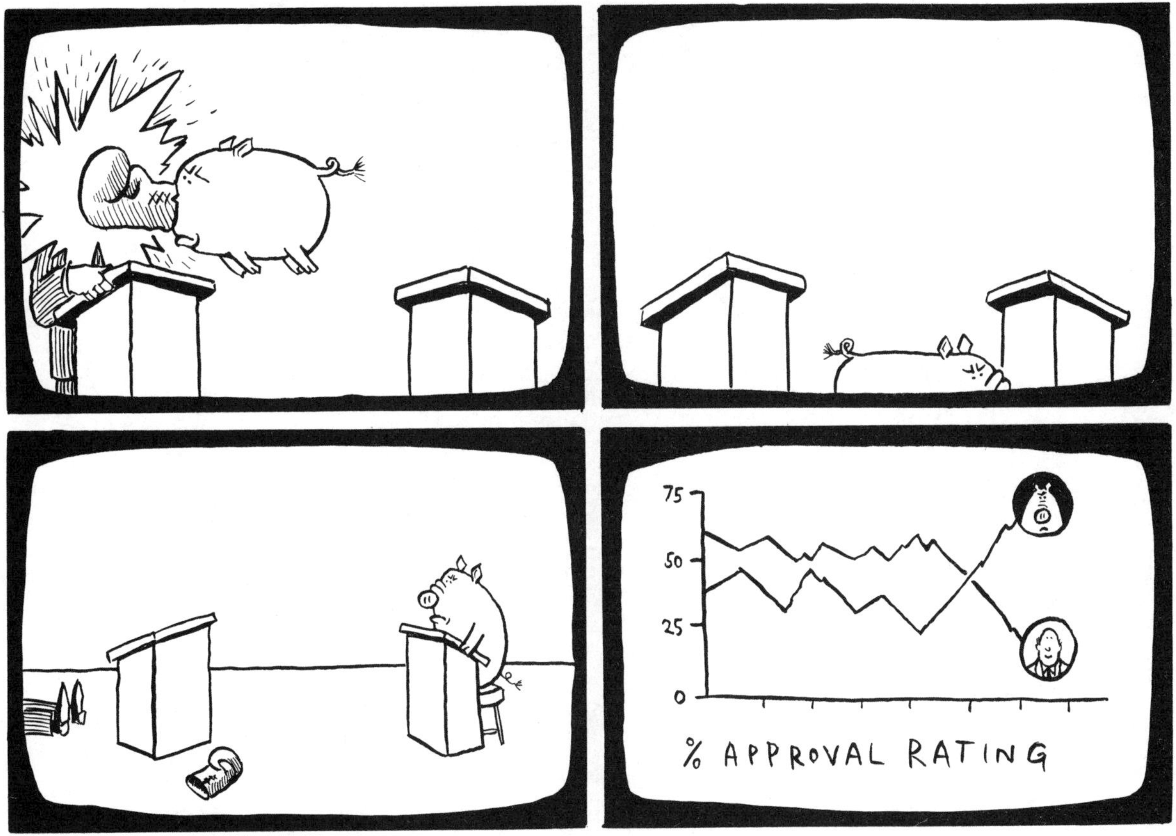
75
50
25
0
% APPROVAL RATING

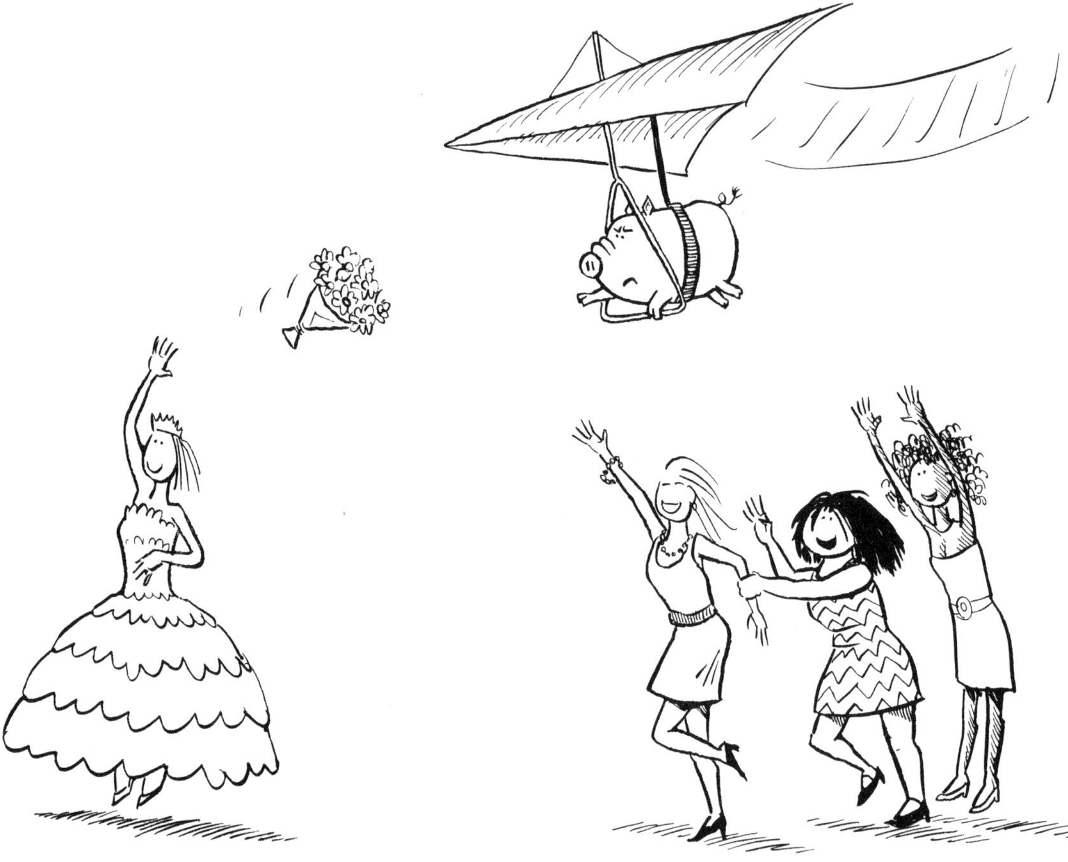

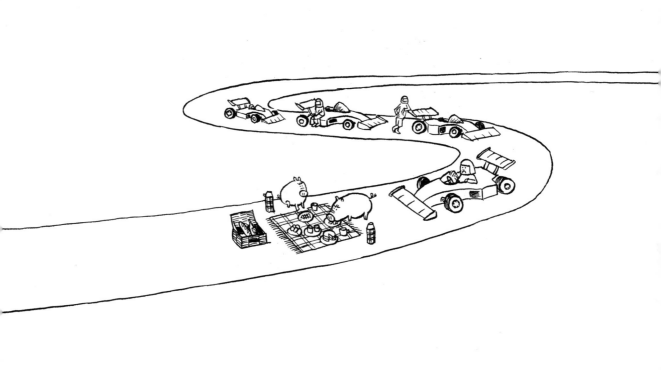

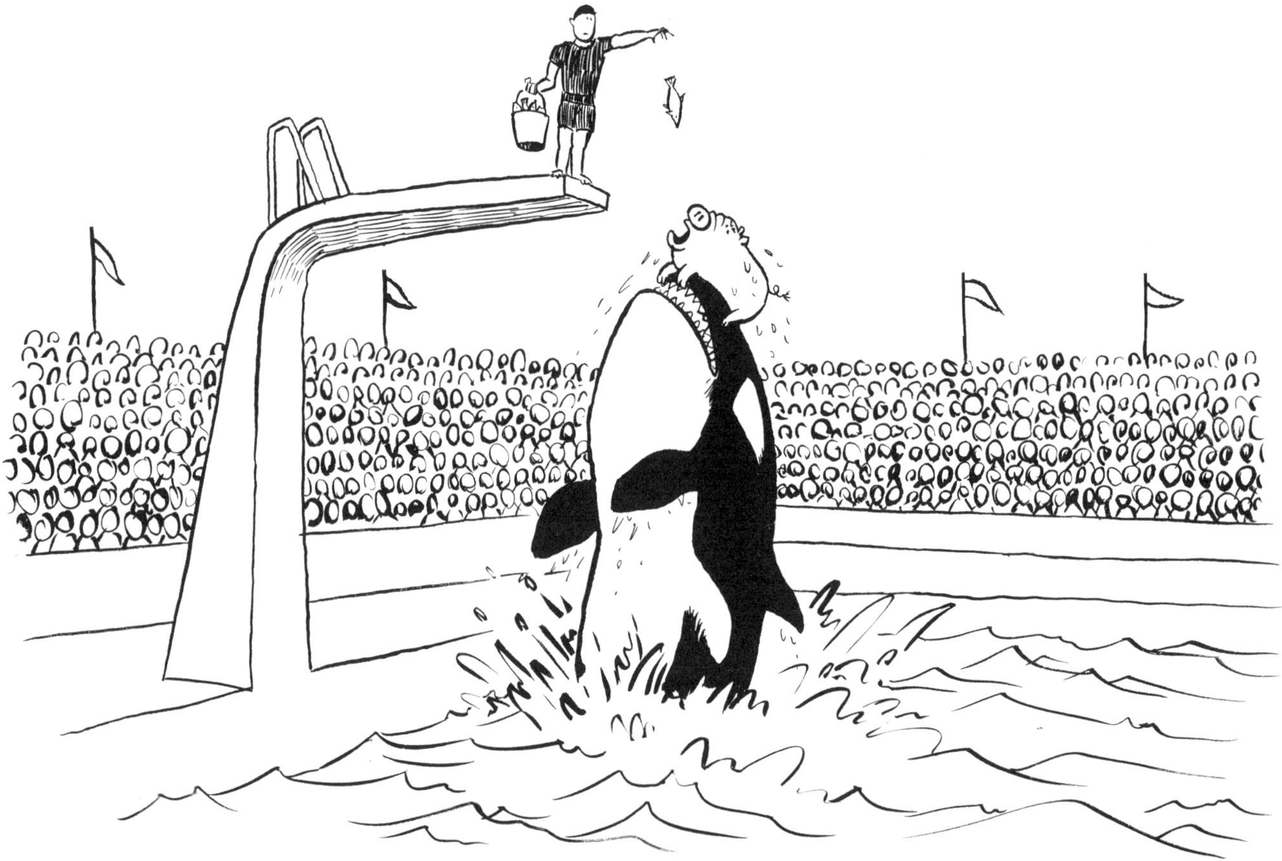

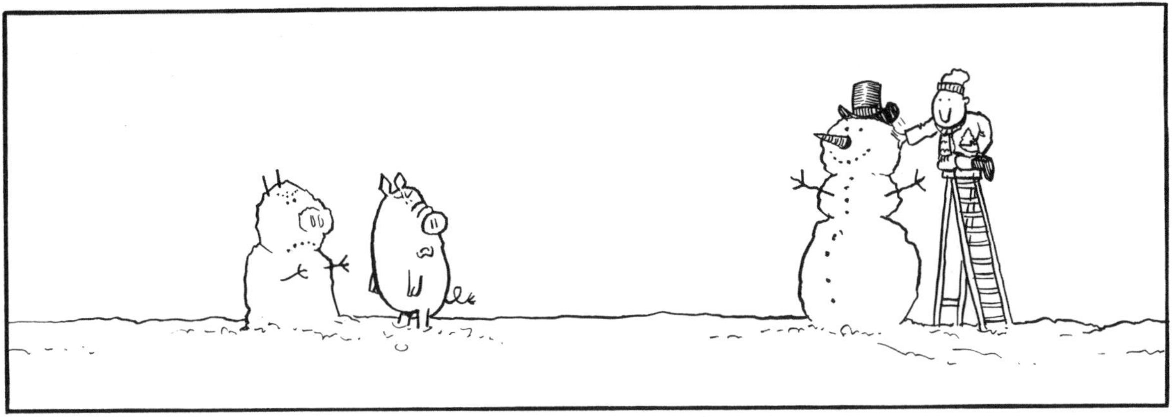

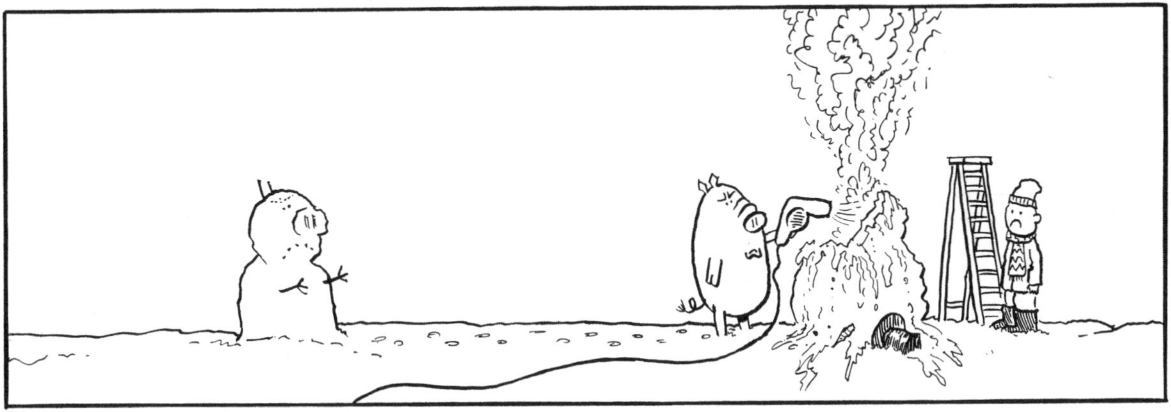

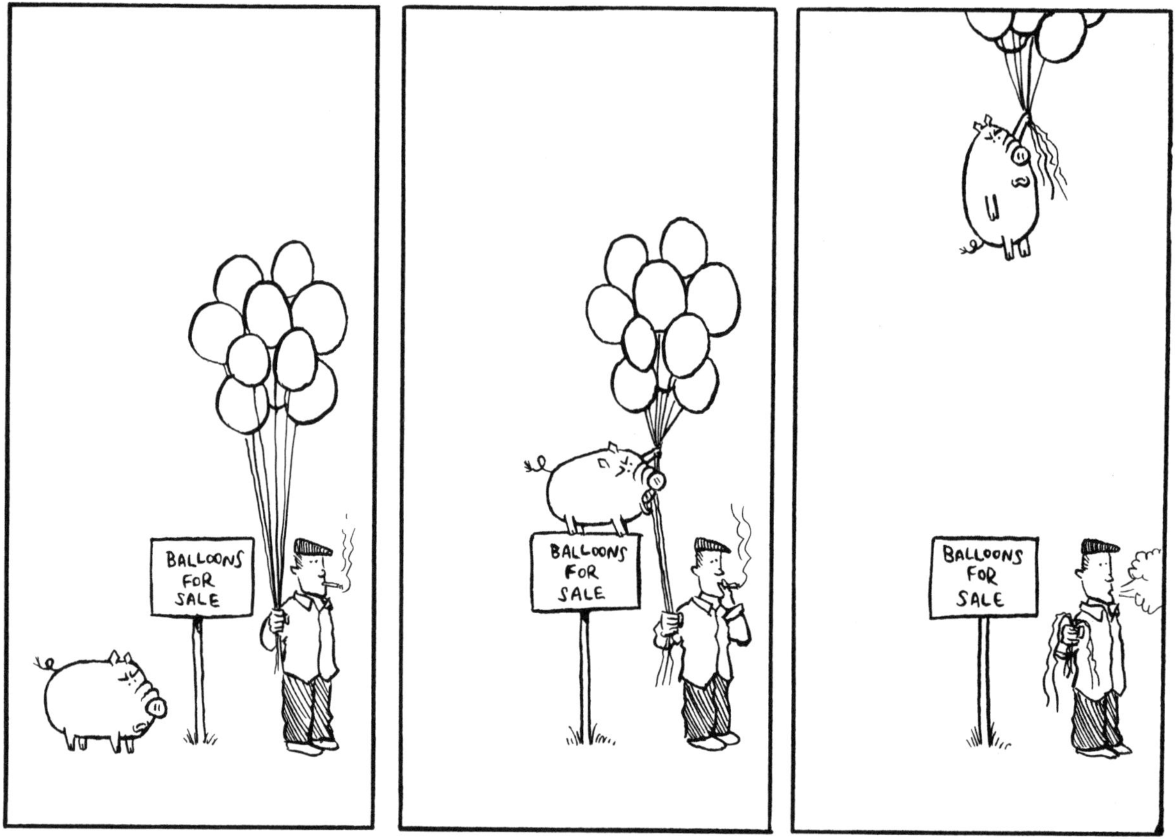
BALLOONS FOR SALE
BALLOONS FOR SALE
BALLOONS FOR SALE

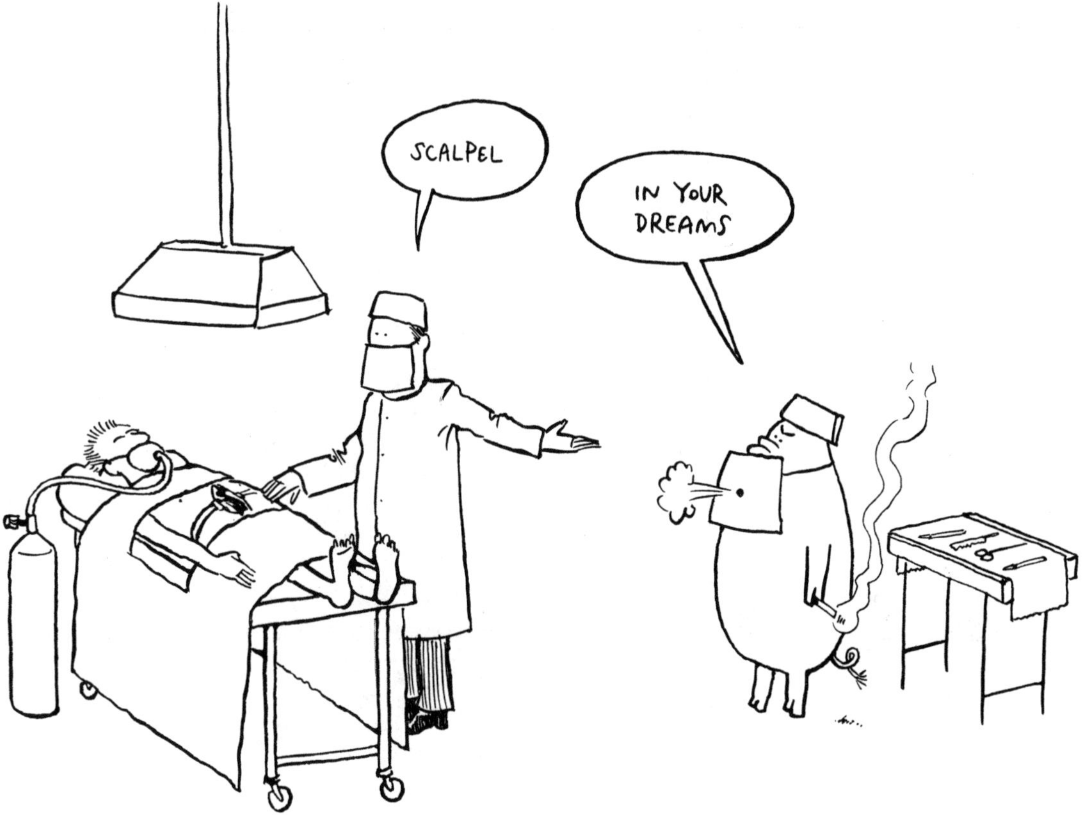
SCALPEL
IN YOUR DREAMS

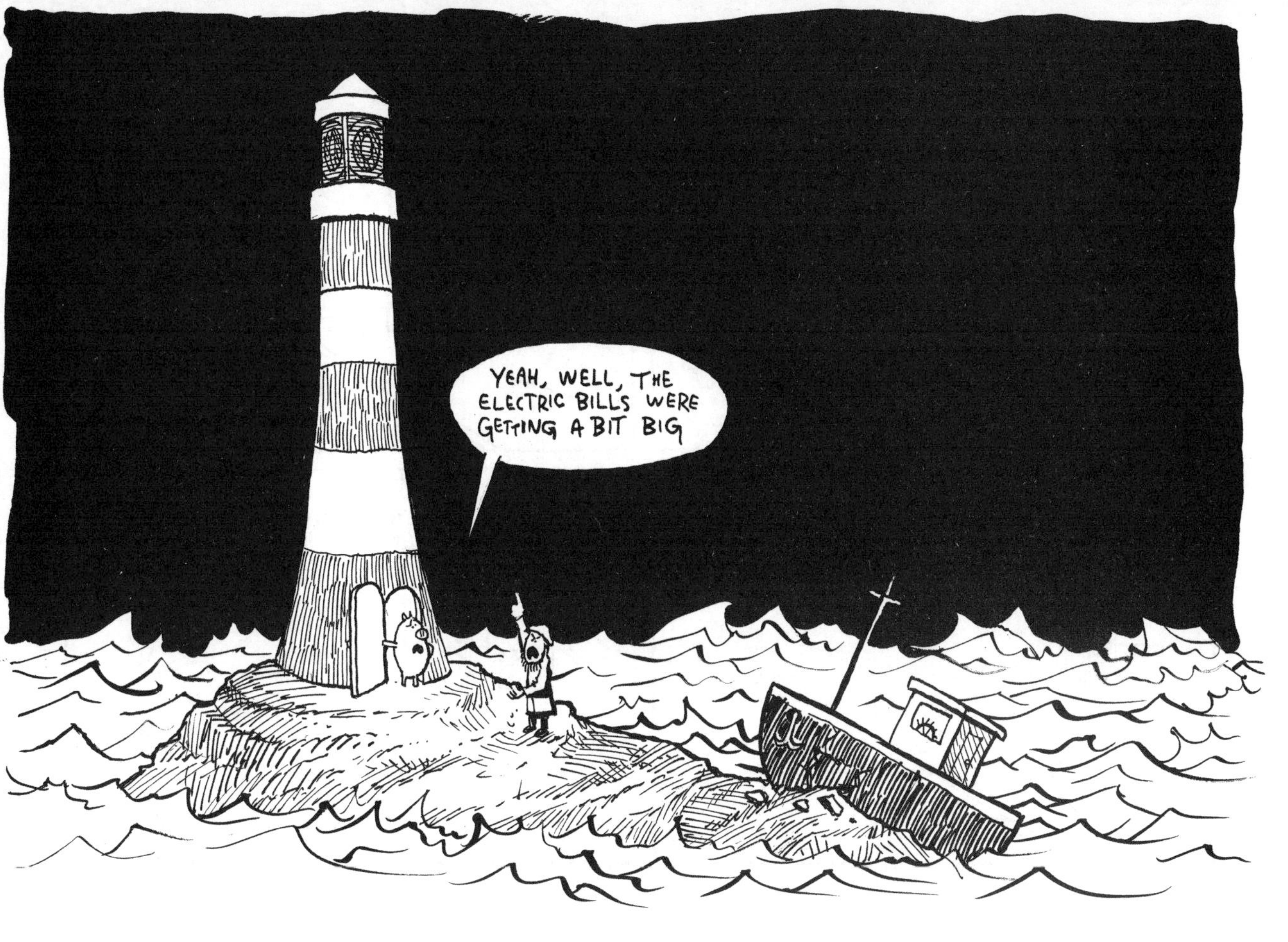
YEAH, WELL, THE ELECTRIC BILLS WERE GETTING A BIT BIG

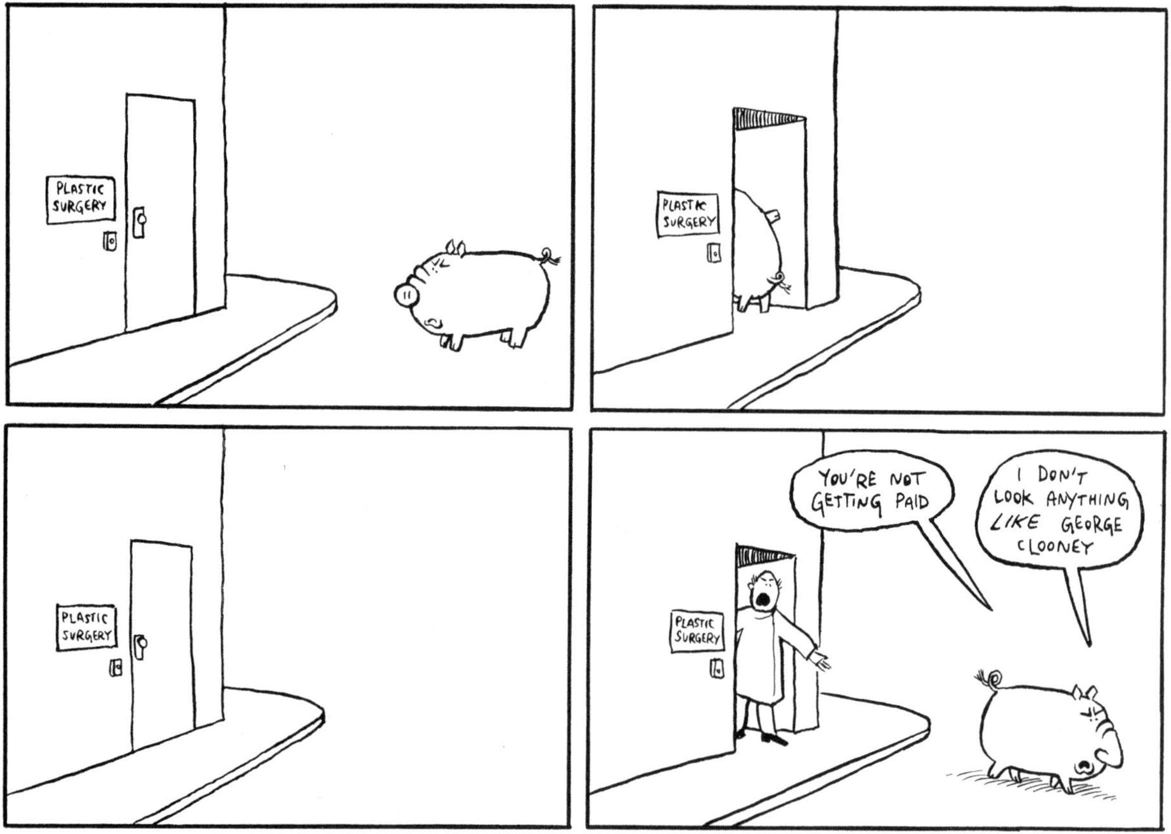
PLASTIC SURGERY
PLASTIC SURGERY
PLASTIC SURGERY
PLASTIC SURGERY
YOU'RE NOT GETTING PAID
I DON'T LOOK ANYTHING LIKE GEORGE CLOONEY

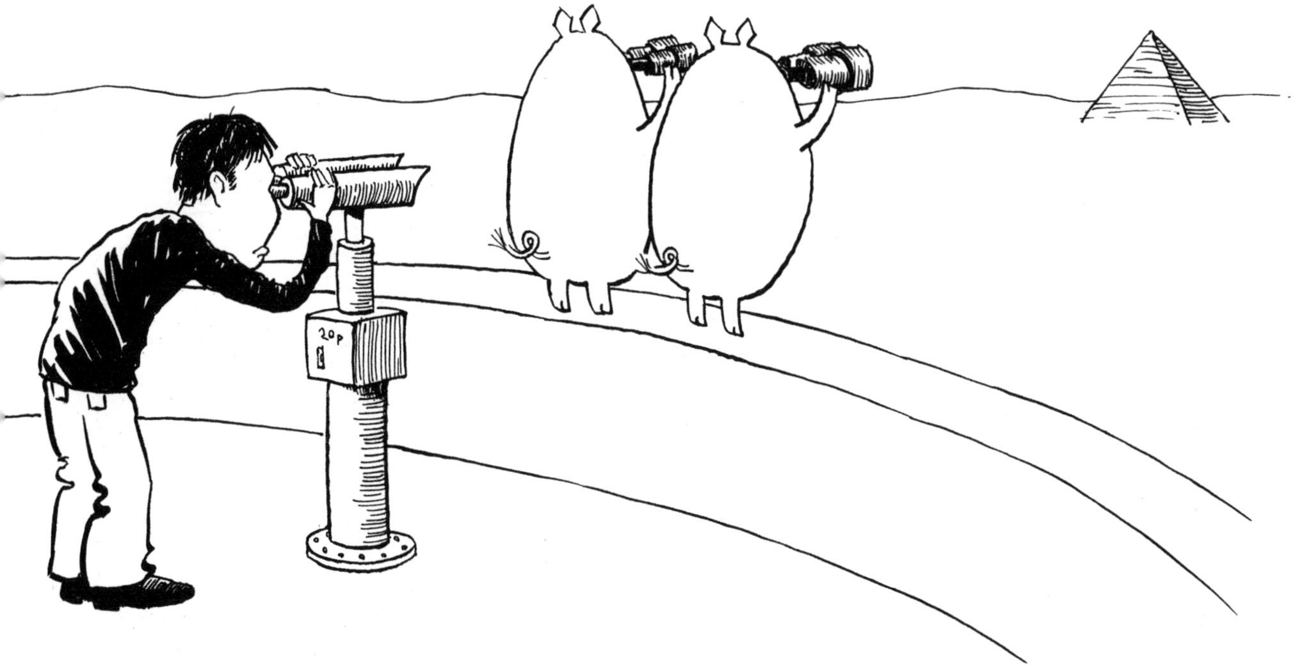
20p

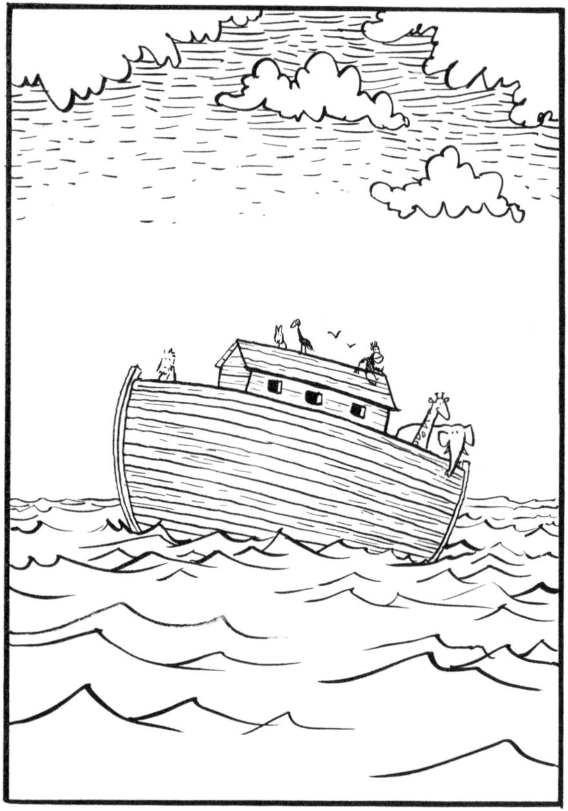

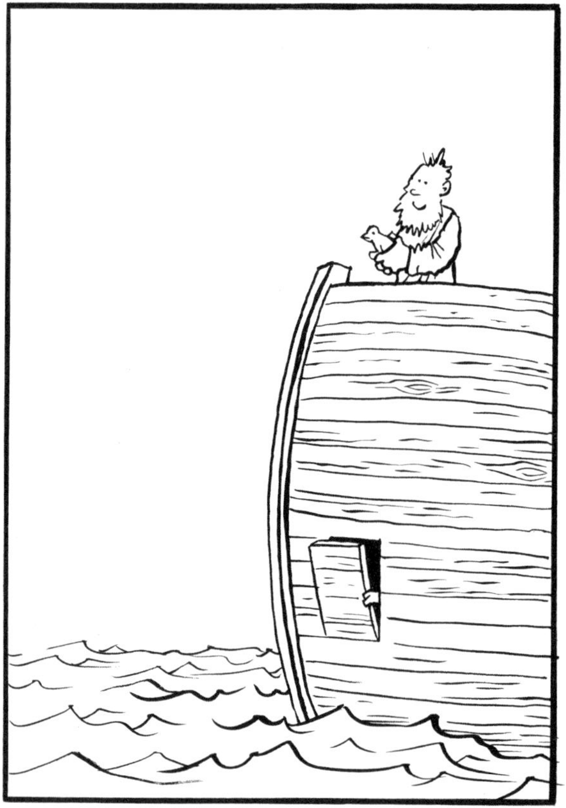

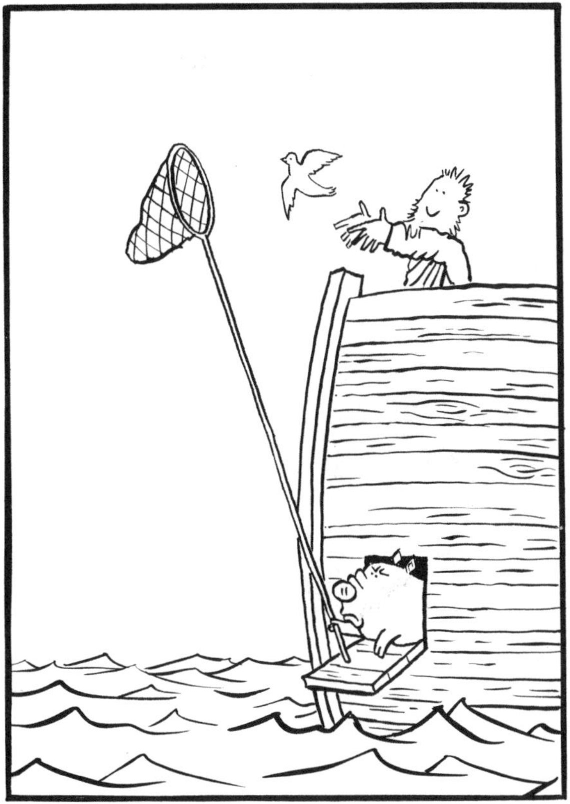
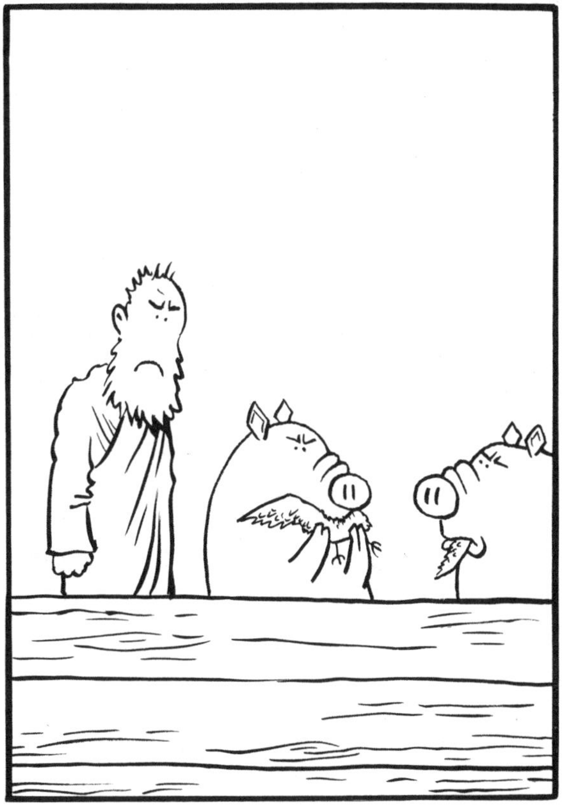

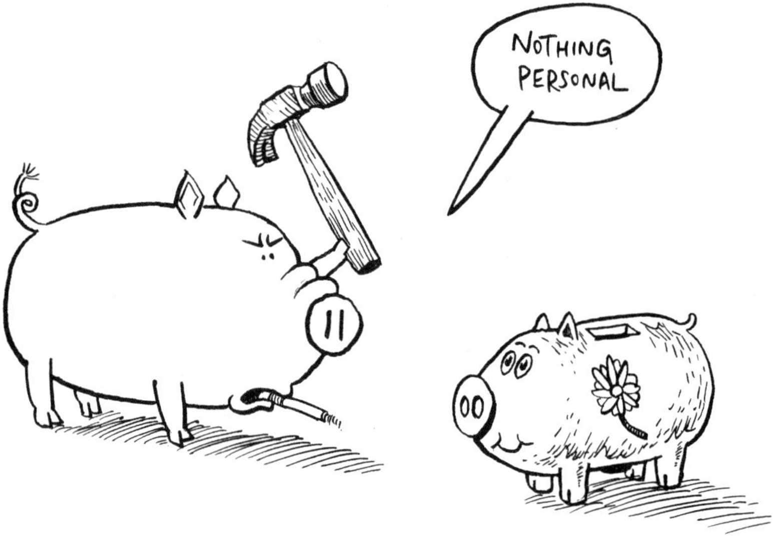
NOTHING PERSONAL

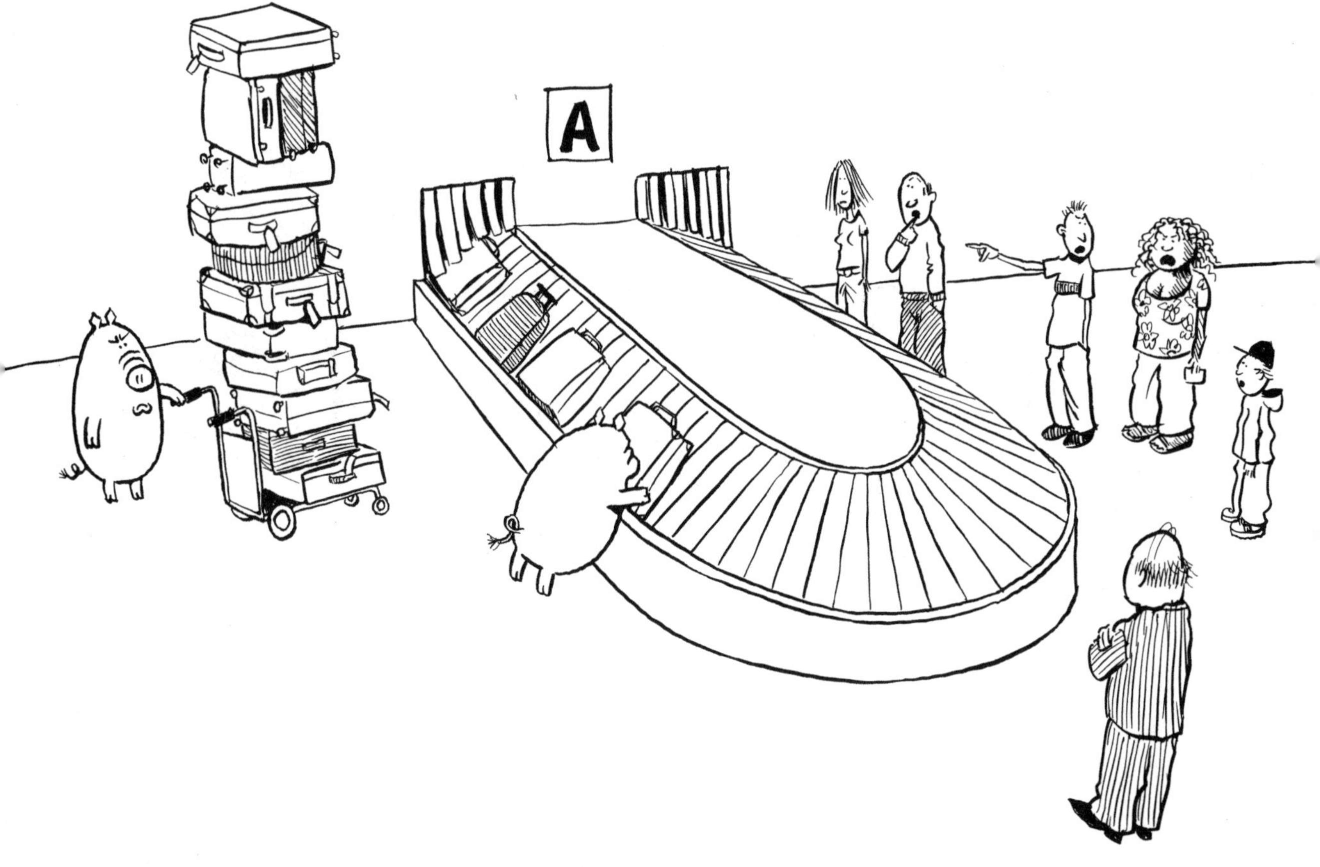
A

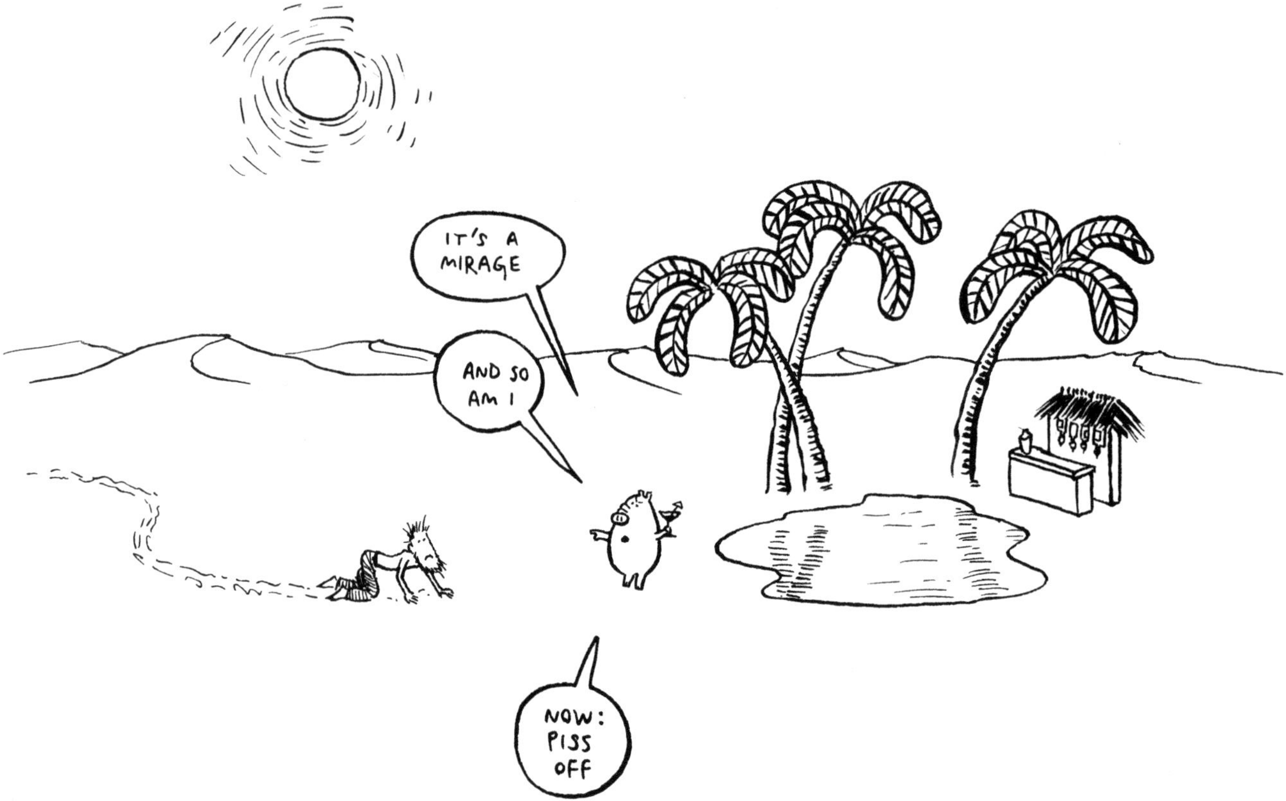
IT'S A MIRAGE
AND SO AM I
NOW: PISS OFF

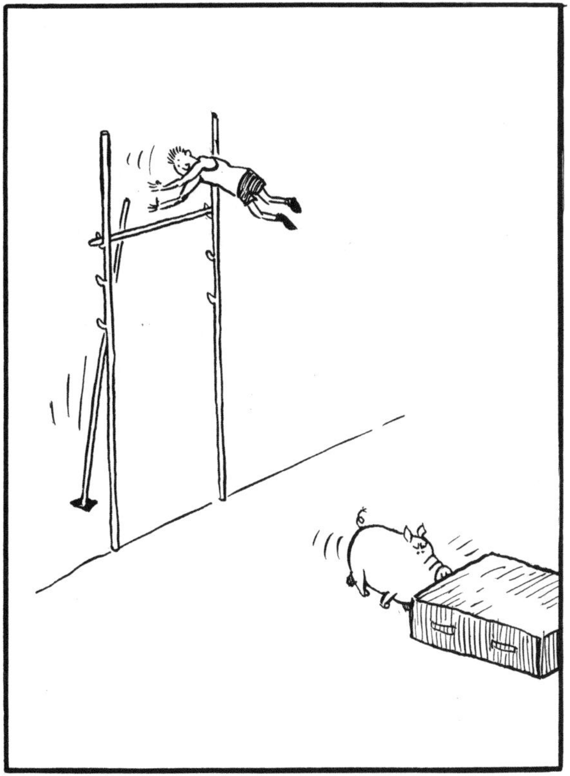

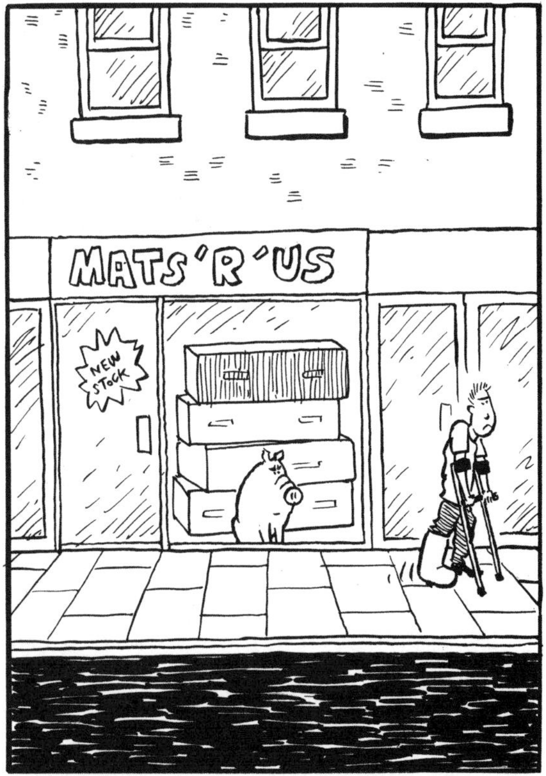
MATS'R'US
NEW STOCK

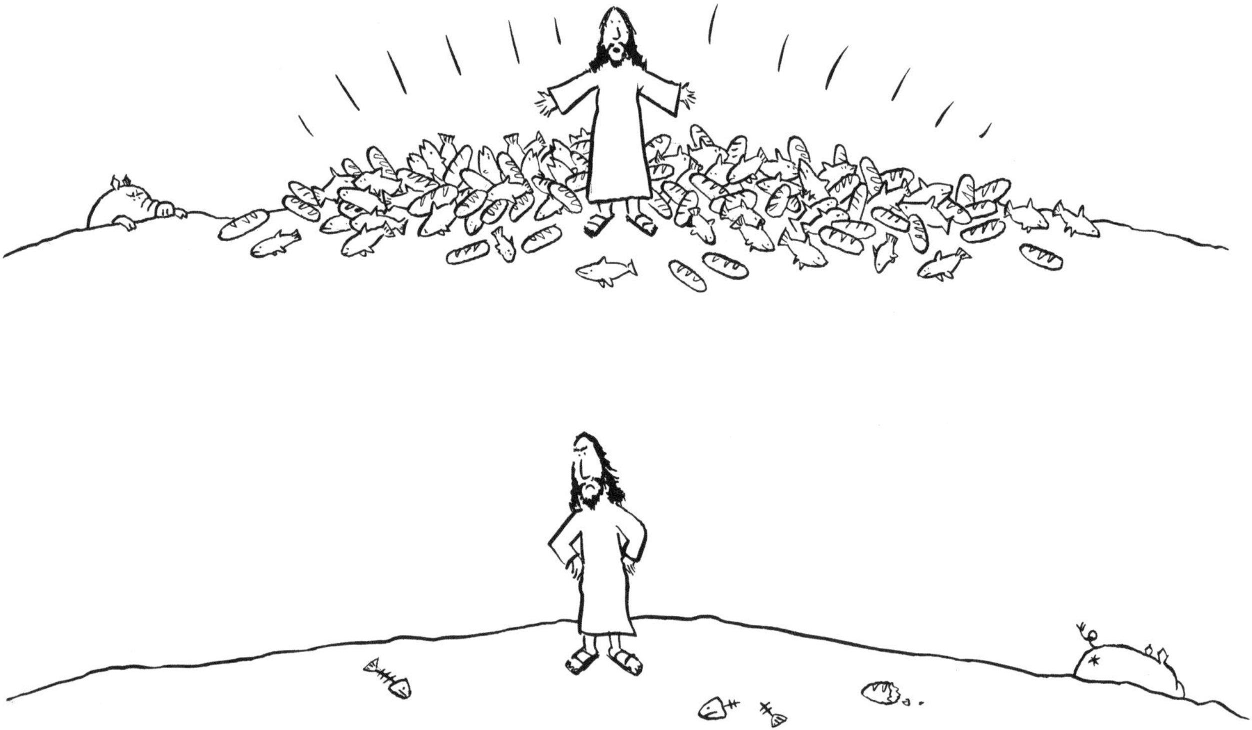

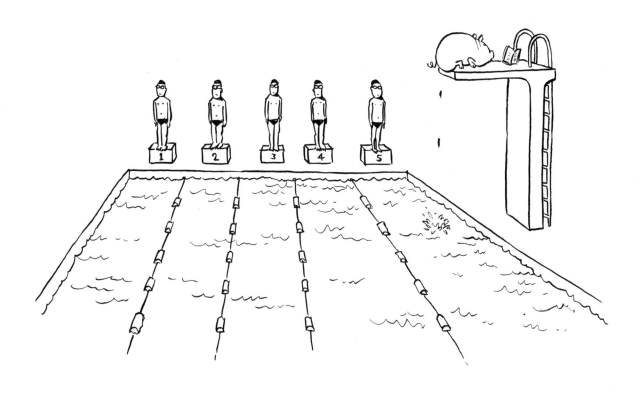

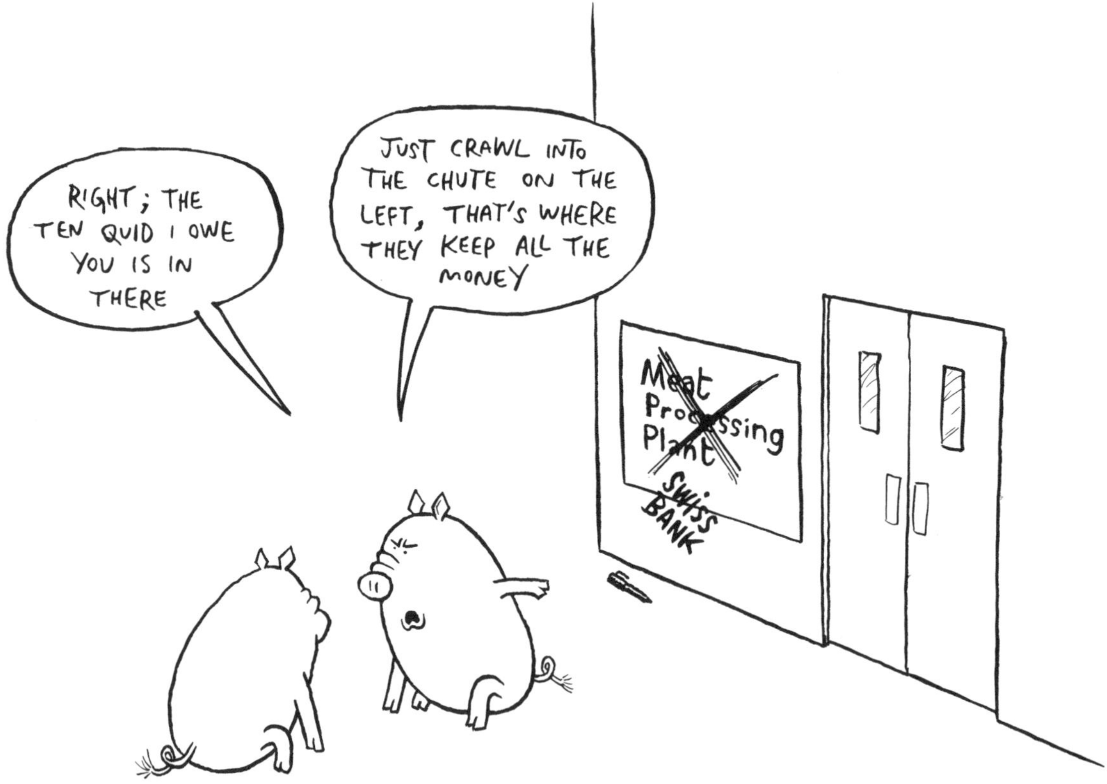
RIGHT; THE TEN QUID I OWE YOU IS IN THERE
JUST CRAWL INTO THE CHUTE ON THE LEFT, THAT'S WHERE THEY KEEP ALL THE MONEY
Meat Processing Plant
SWISS BANK

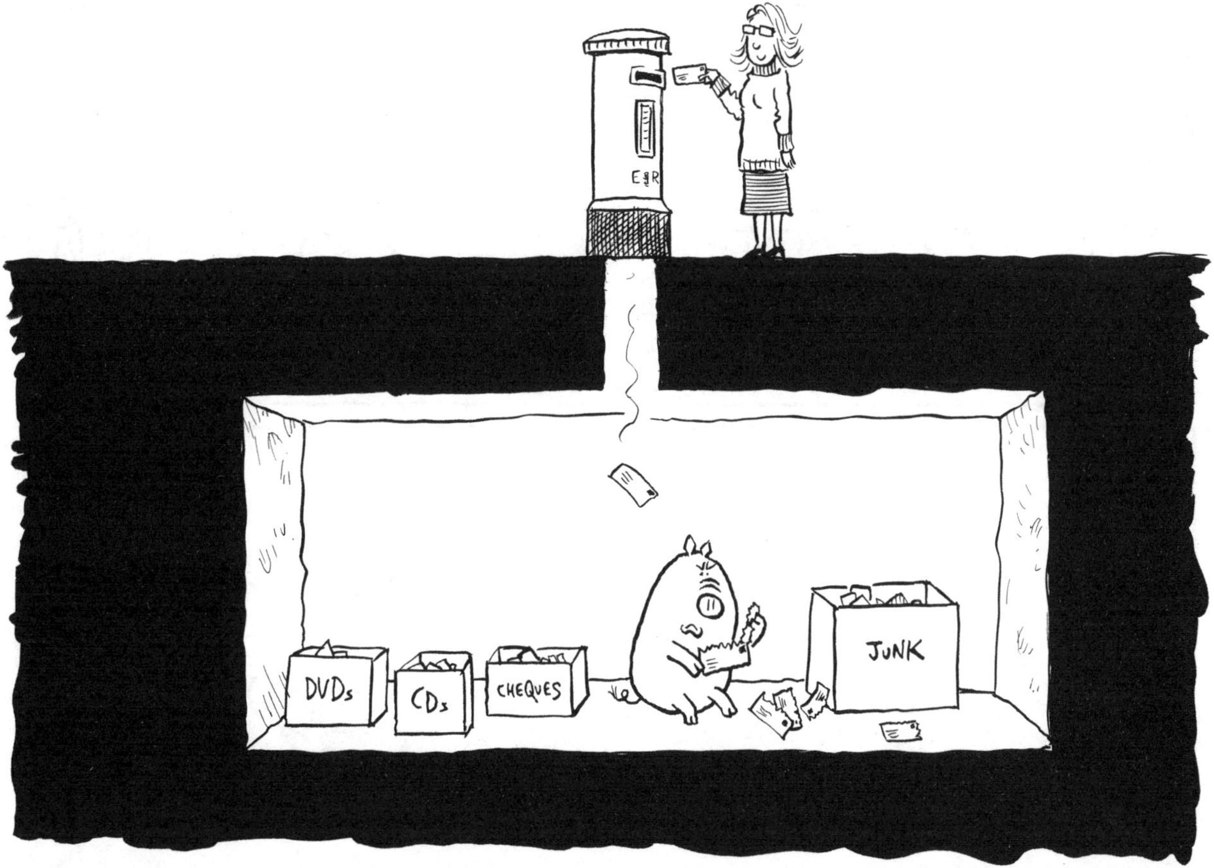
DVDs
CDs
CHEQUES
JUNK

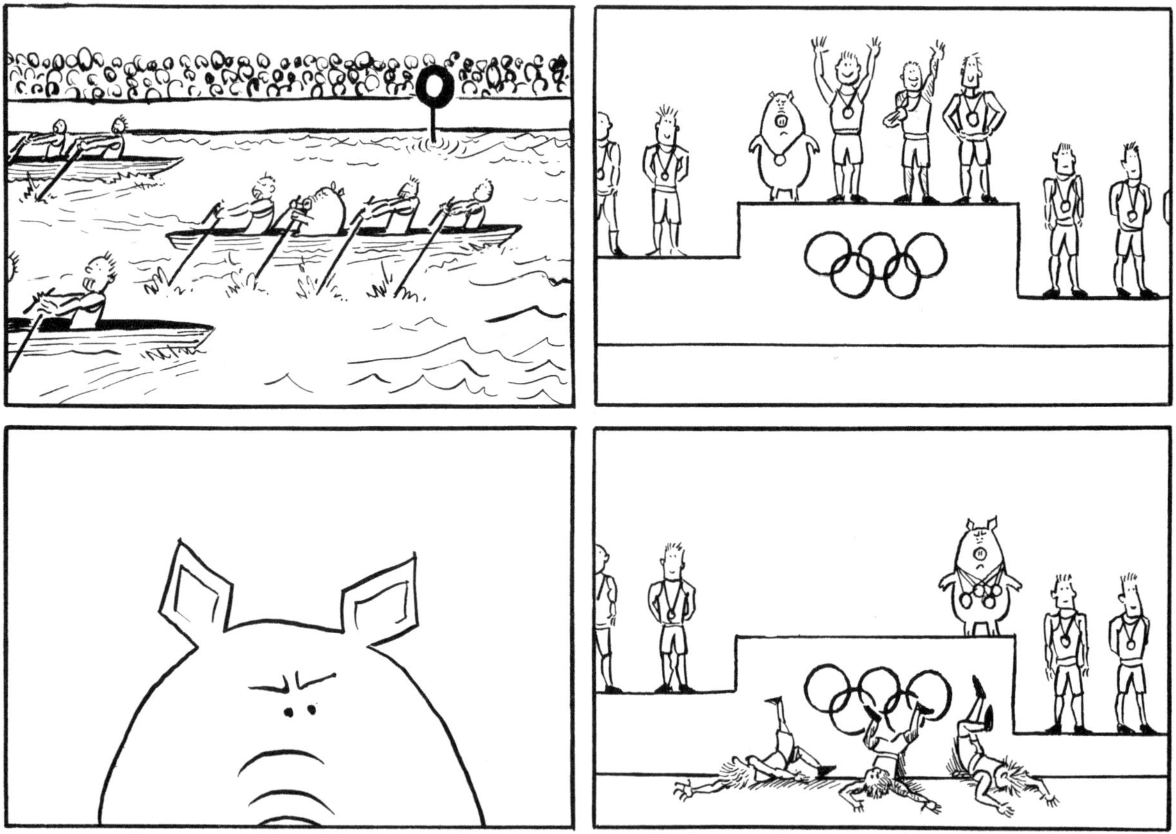

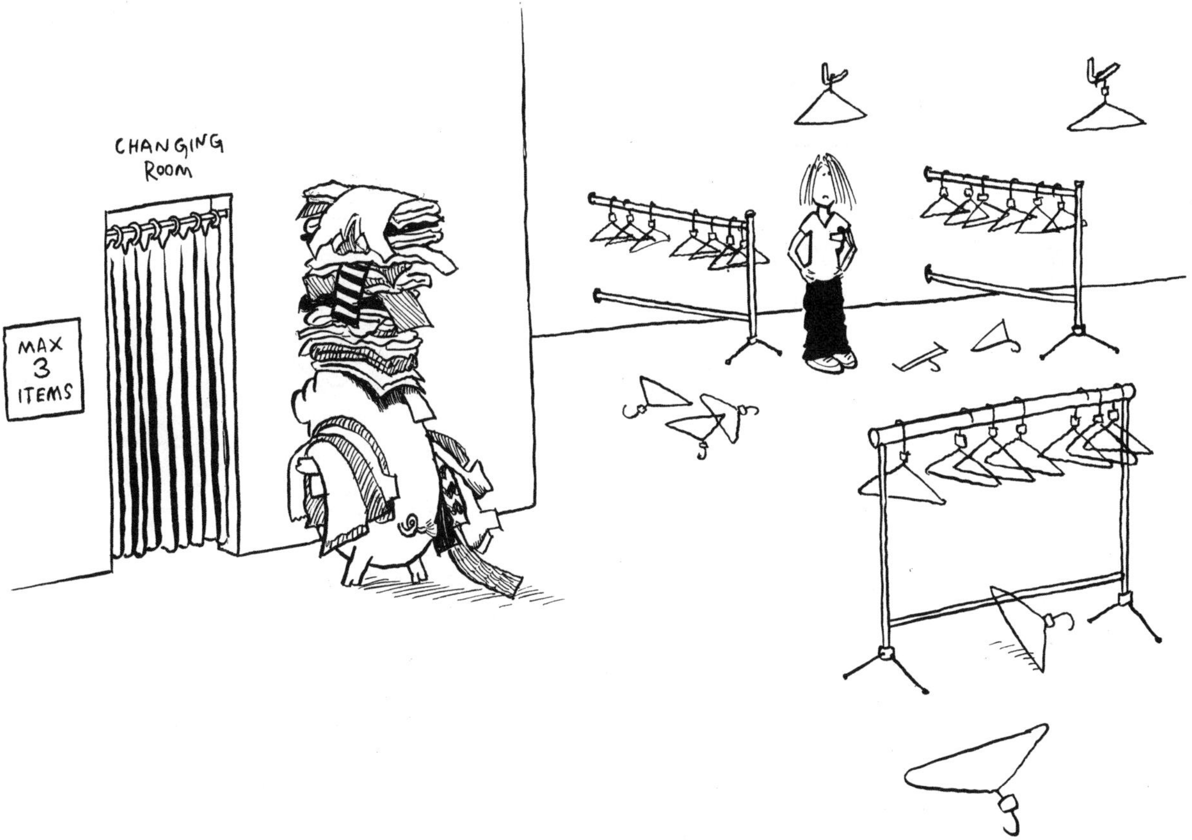
CHANGING ROOM
MAX 3 ITEMS

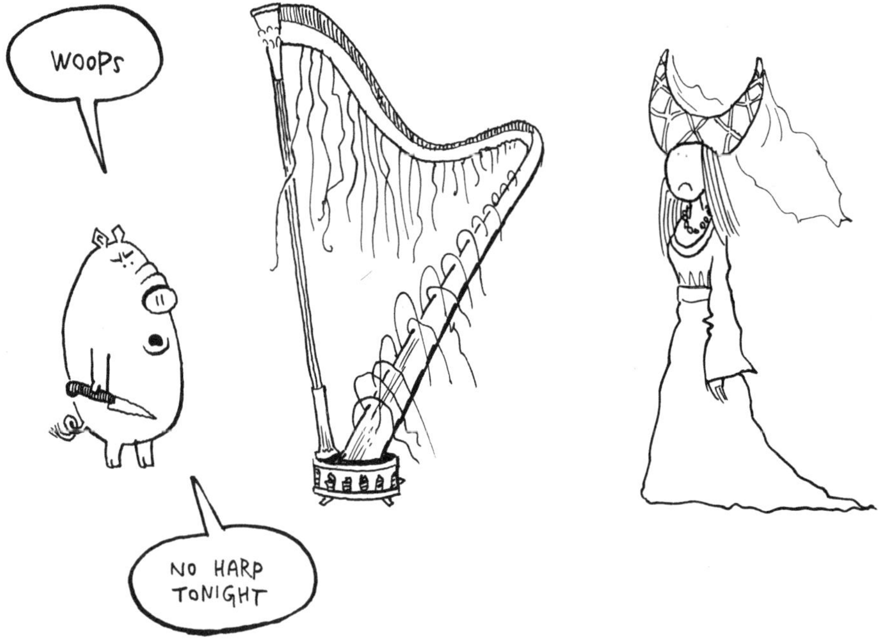
WOOPS
NO HARP TONIGHT

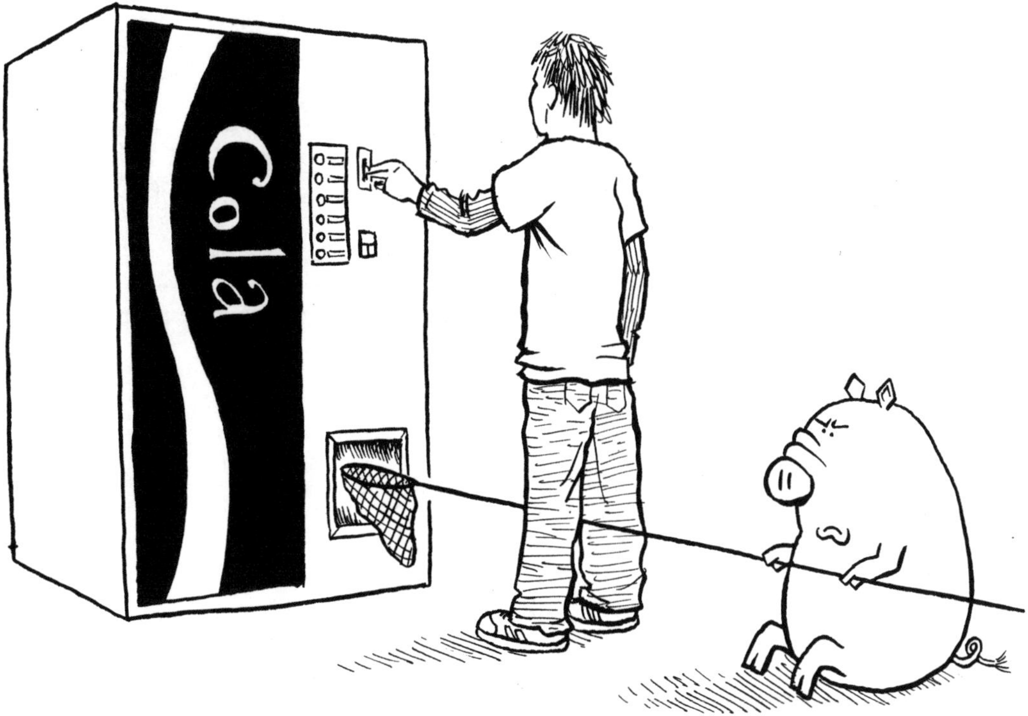
Cola

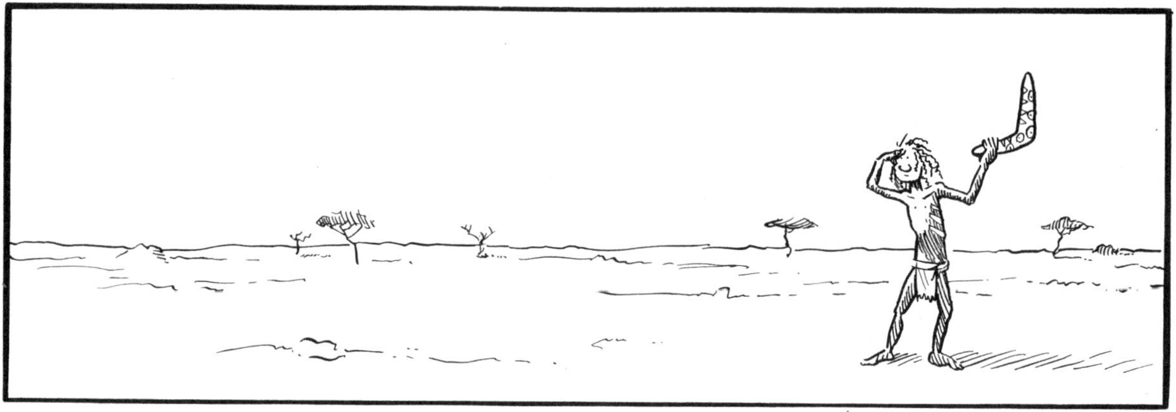

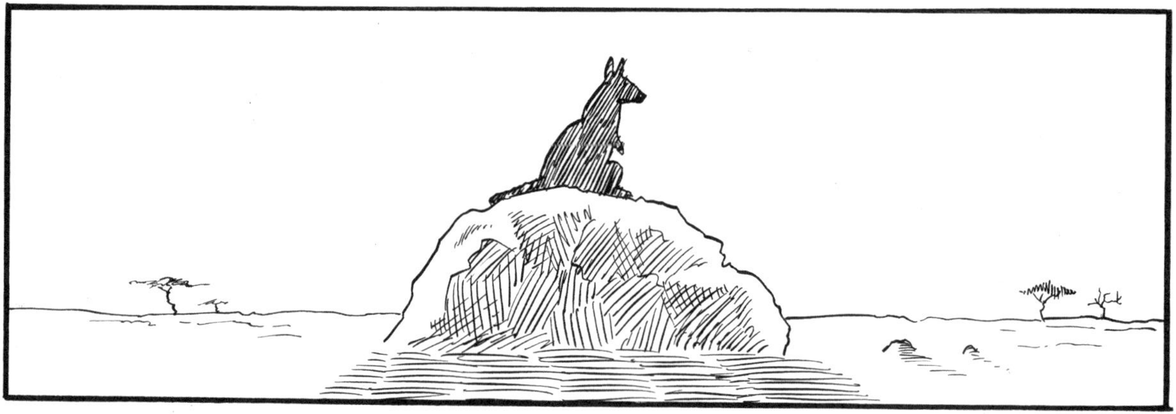

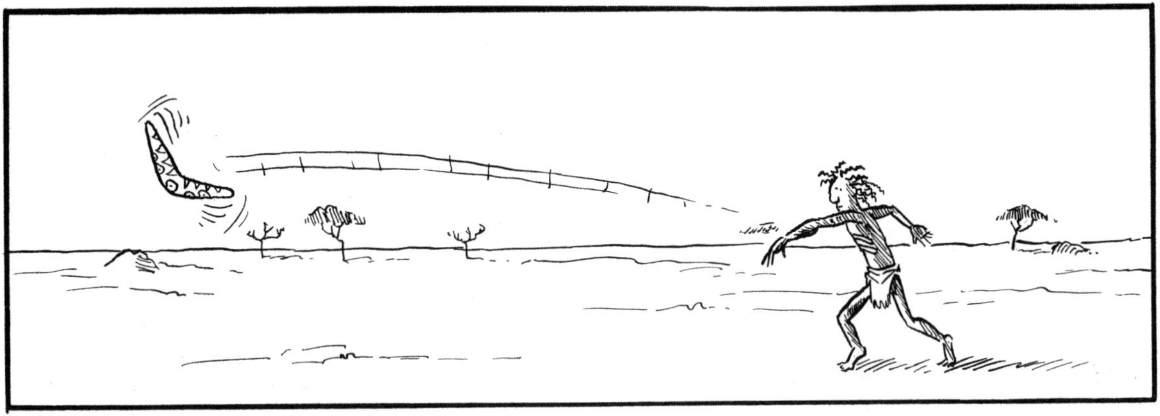

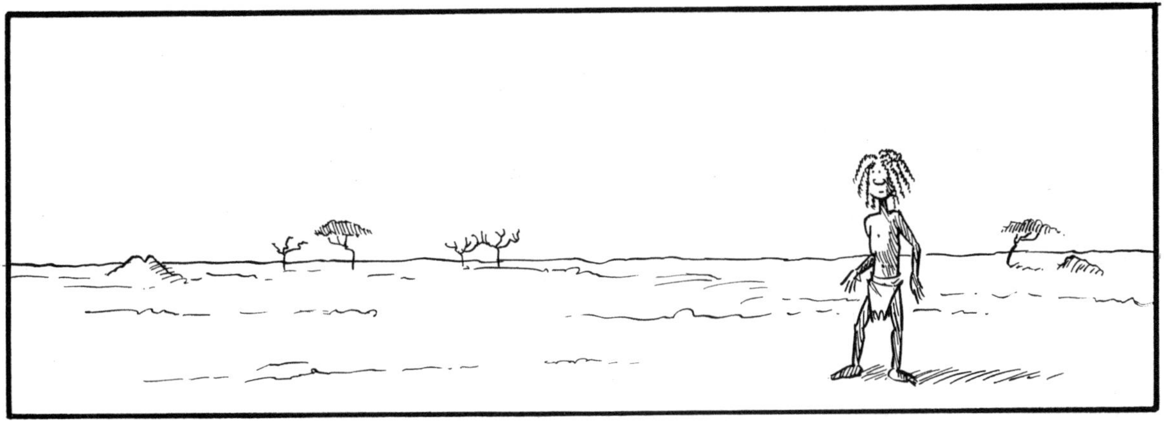

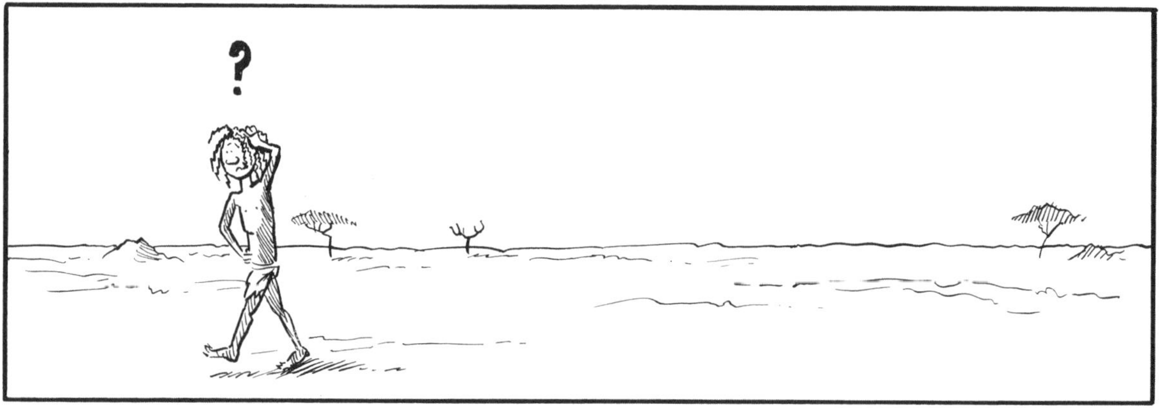
?

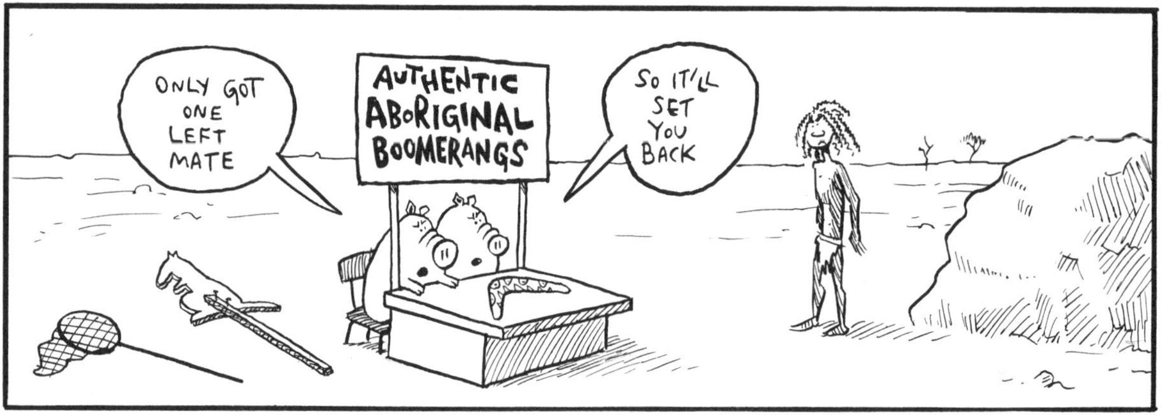
ONLY GOT ONE LEFT MATE
AUTHENTIC ABORIGINAL BOOMERANGS
SO IT'LL SET YOU BACK

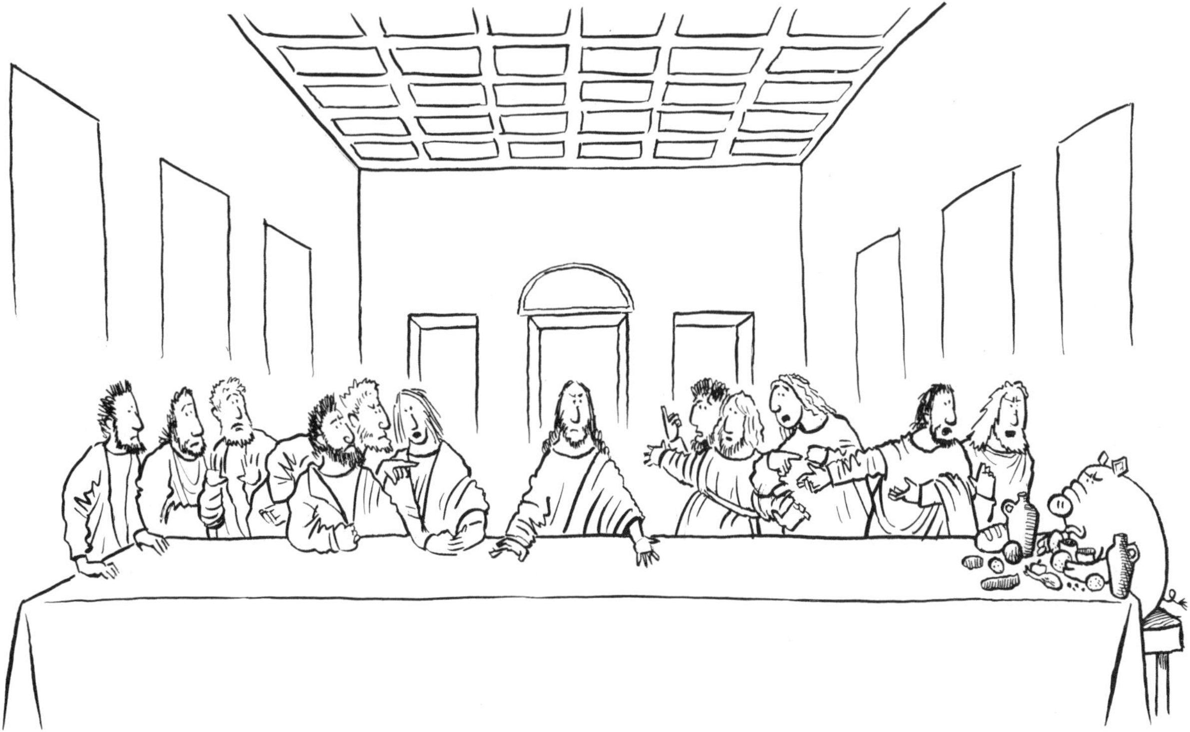

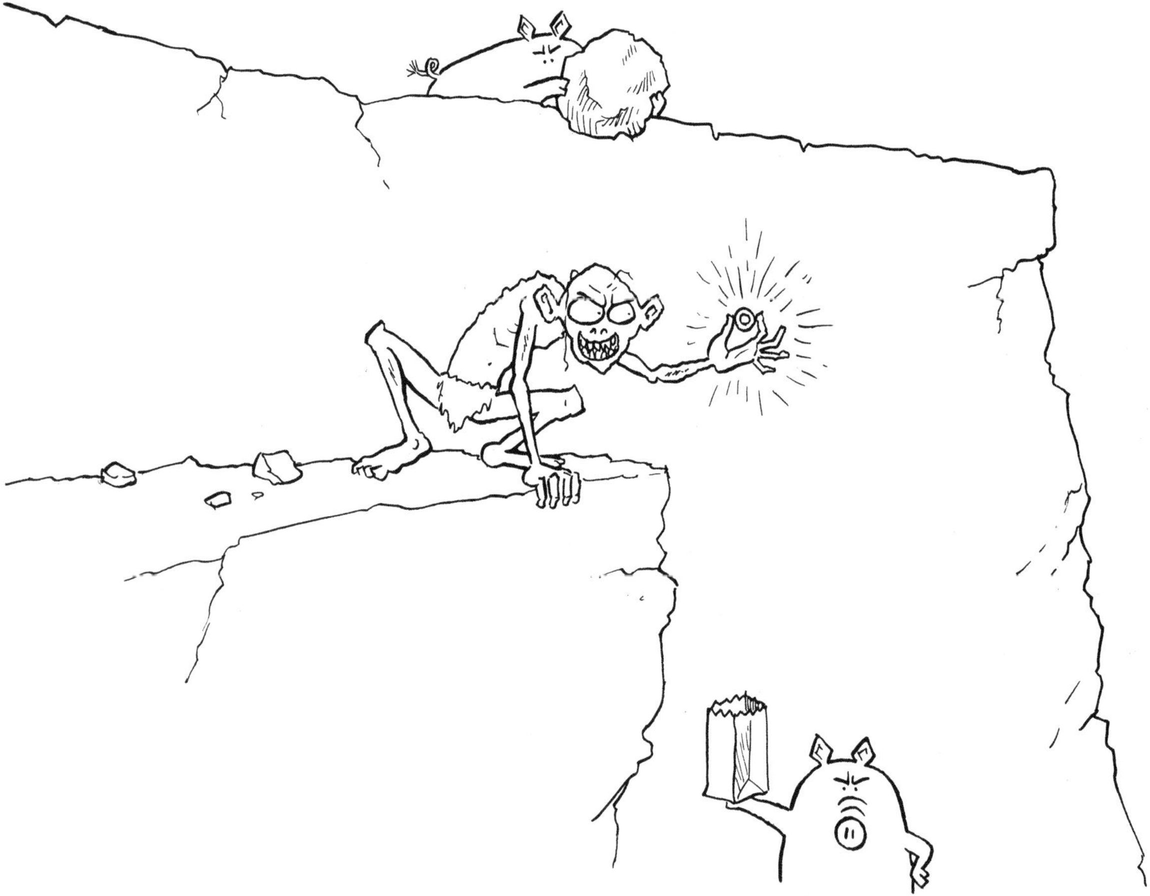

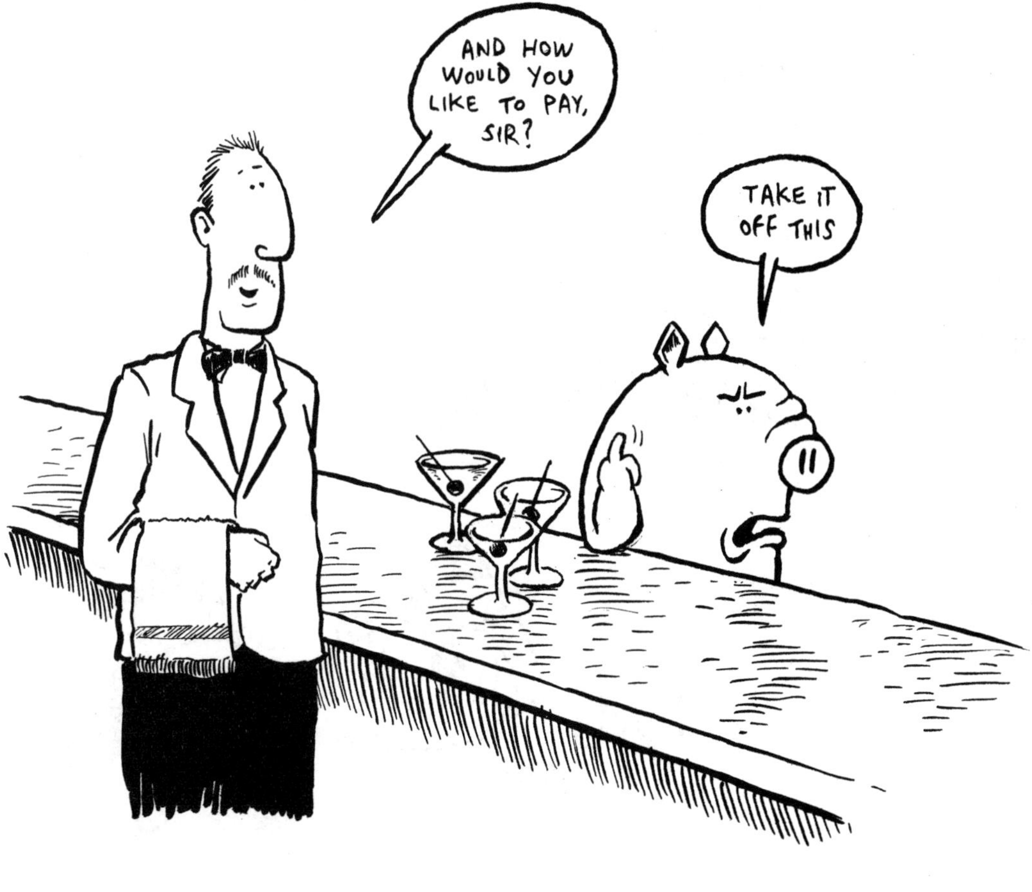
AND HOW WOULD YOU LIKE TO PAY, SIR?
TAKE IT OFF THIS

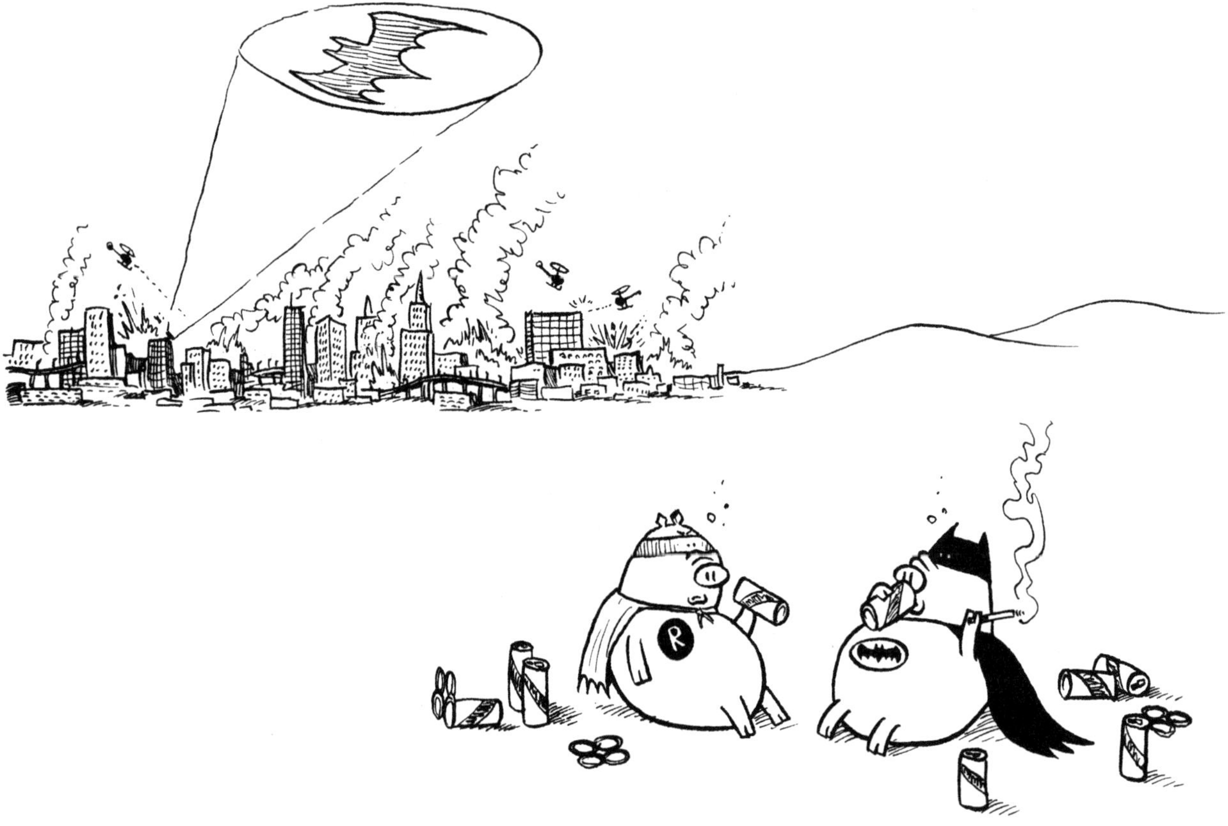

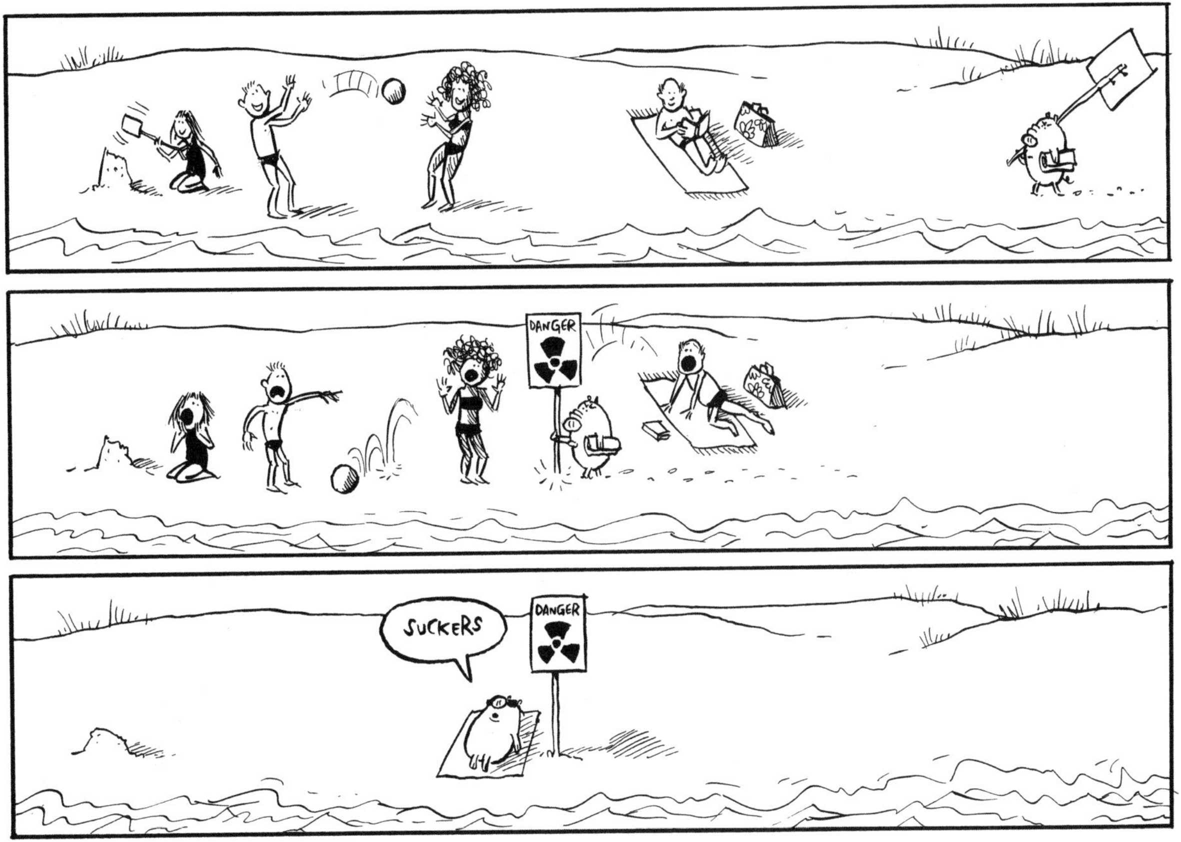
DANGER
DANGER
SUCKERS

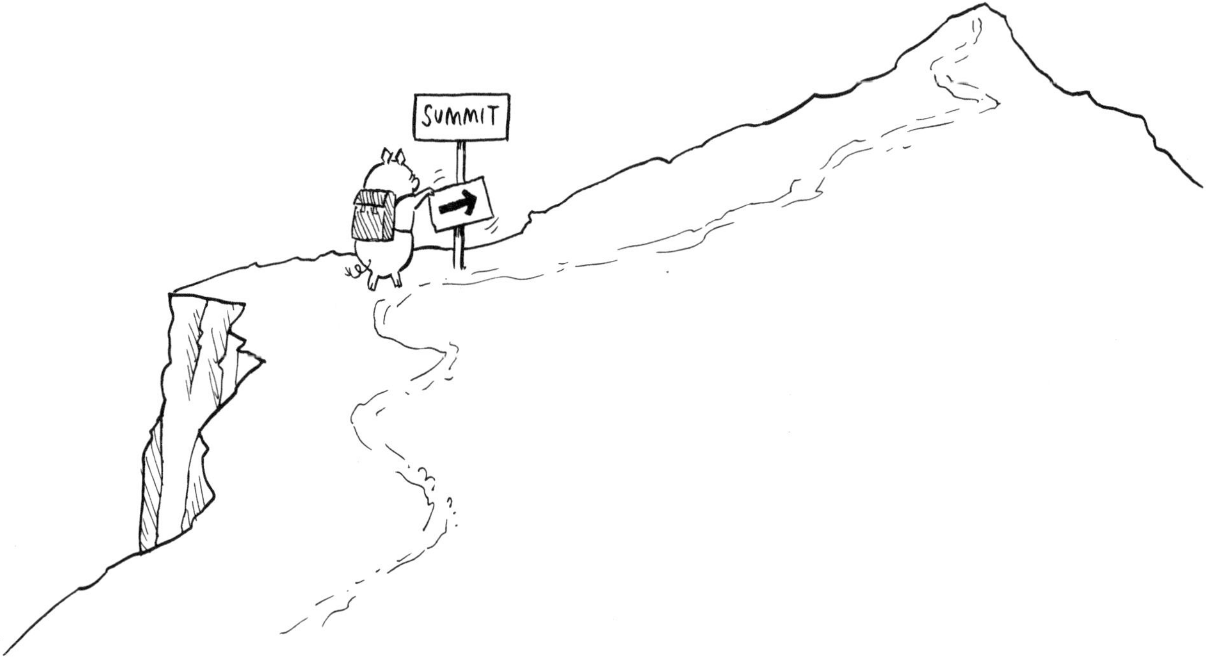
SUMMIT

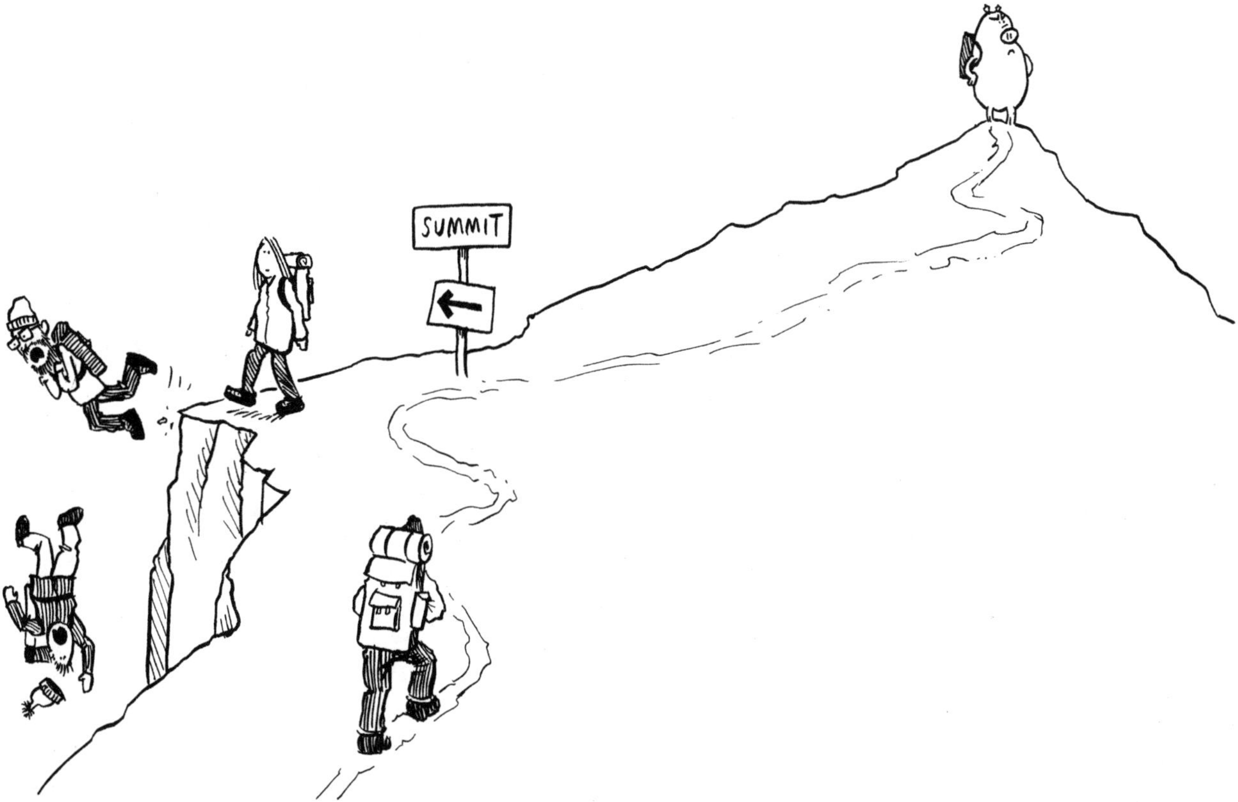
SUMMIT

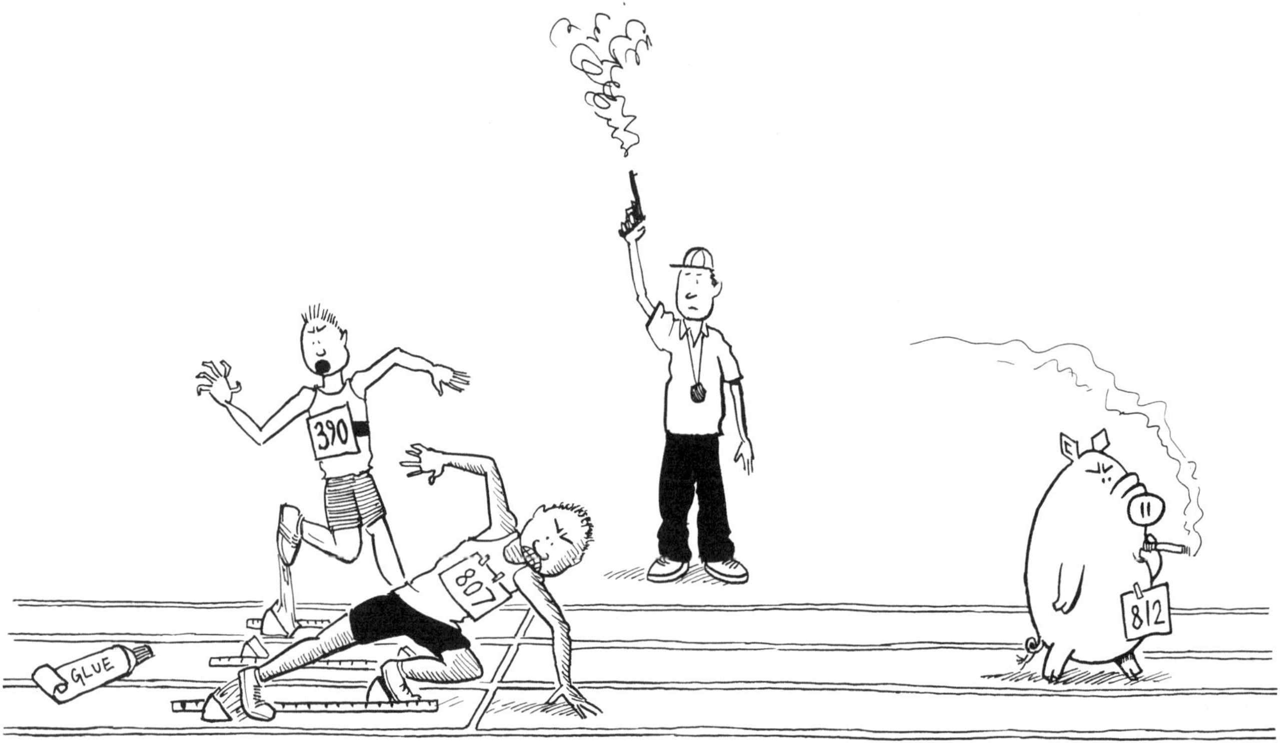
390
807
812
GLUE

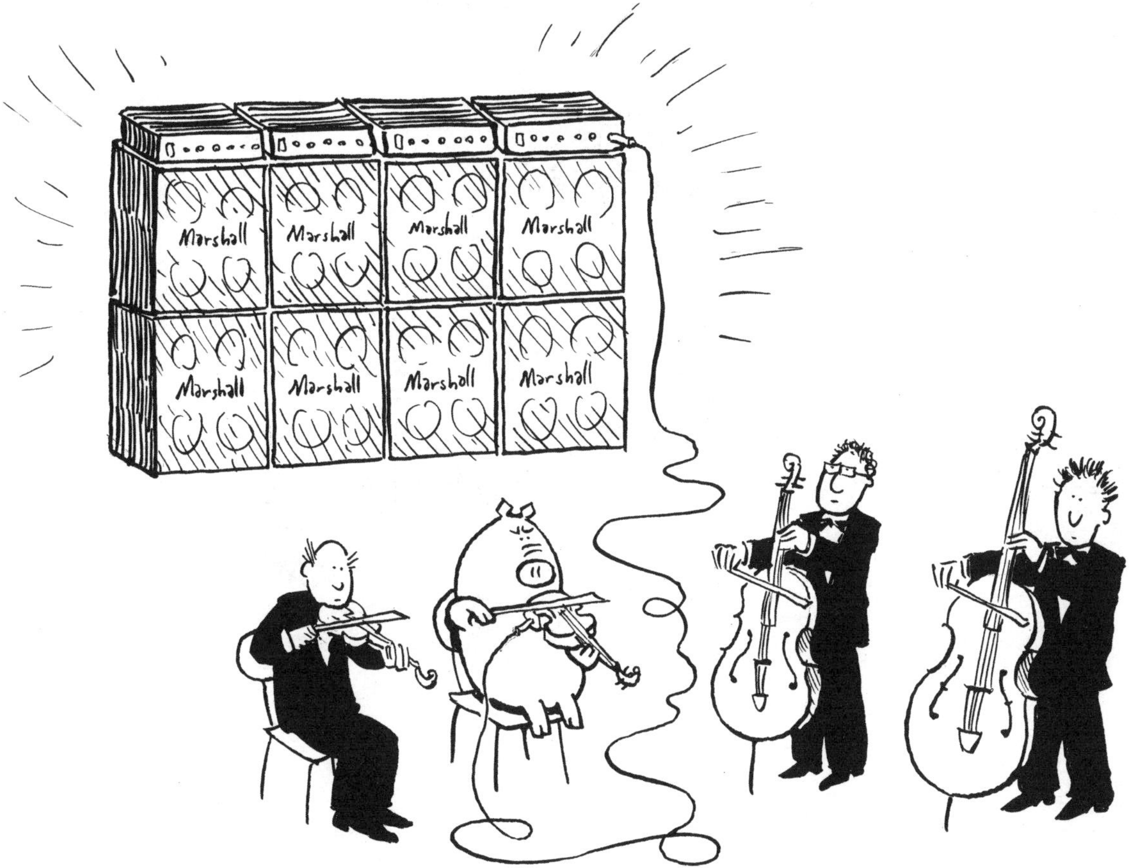
Marshall
Marshall
Marshall
Marshall
Marshall
Marshall
Marshall
Marshall

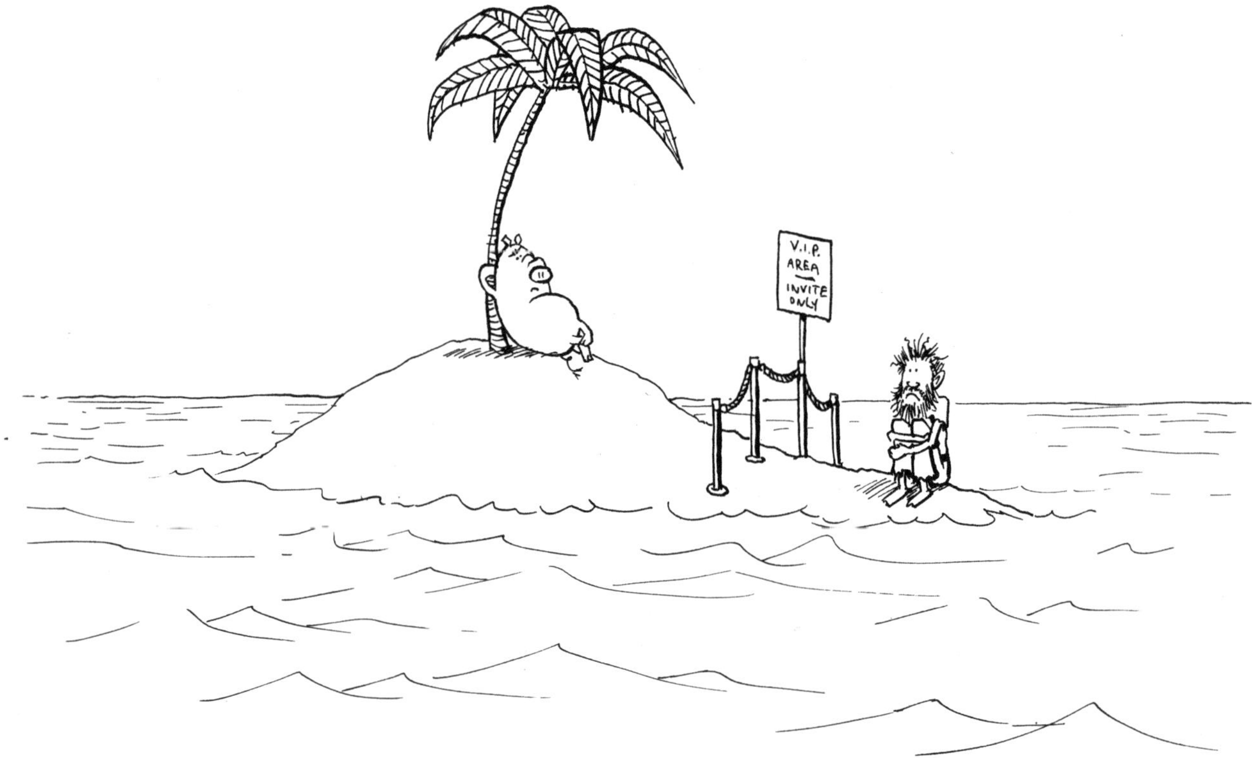
V.I.P.
AREA
INVITE
ONLY

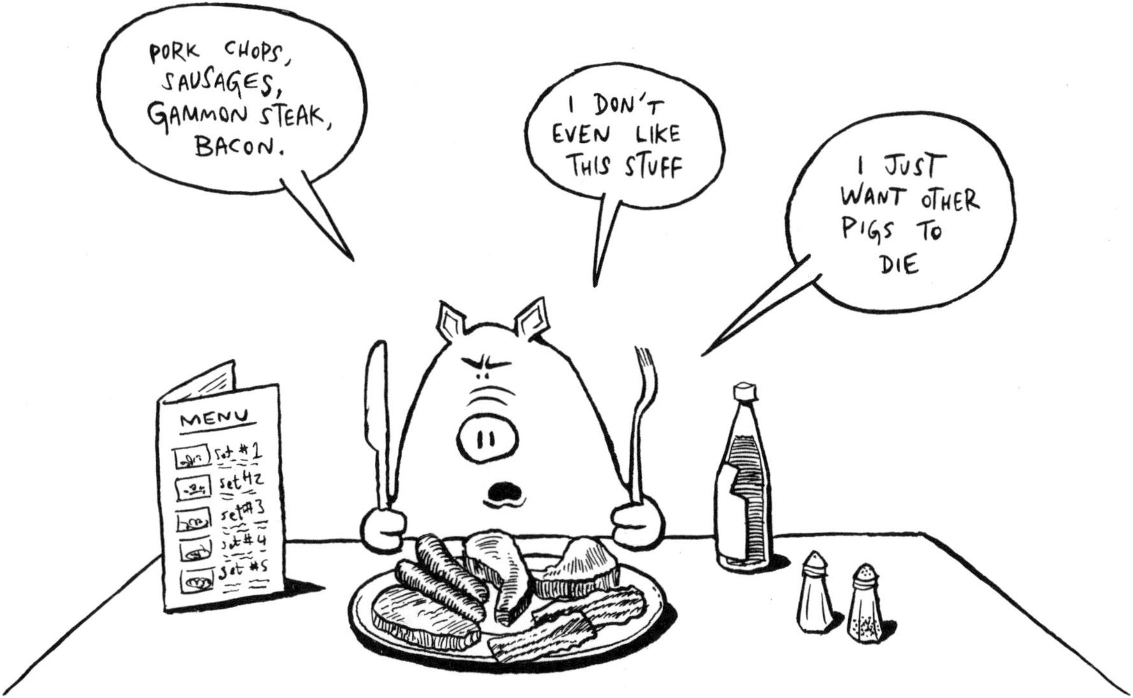
PORK CHOPS, SAUSAGES, GAMMON STEAK, BACON.
I DON'T EVEN LIKE THIS STUFF
I JUST WANT OTHER PIGS TO DIE
MENU

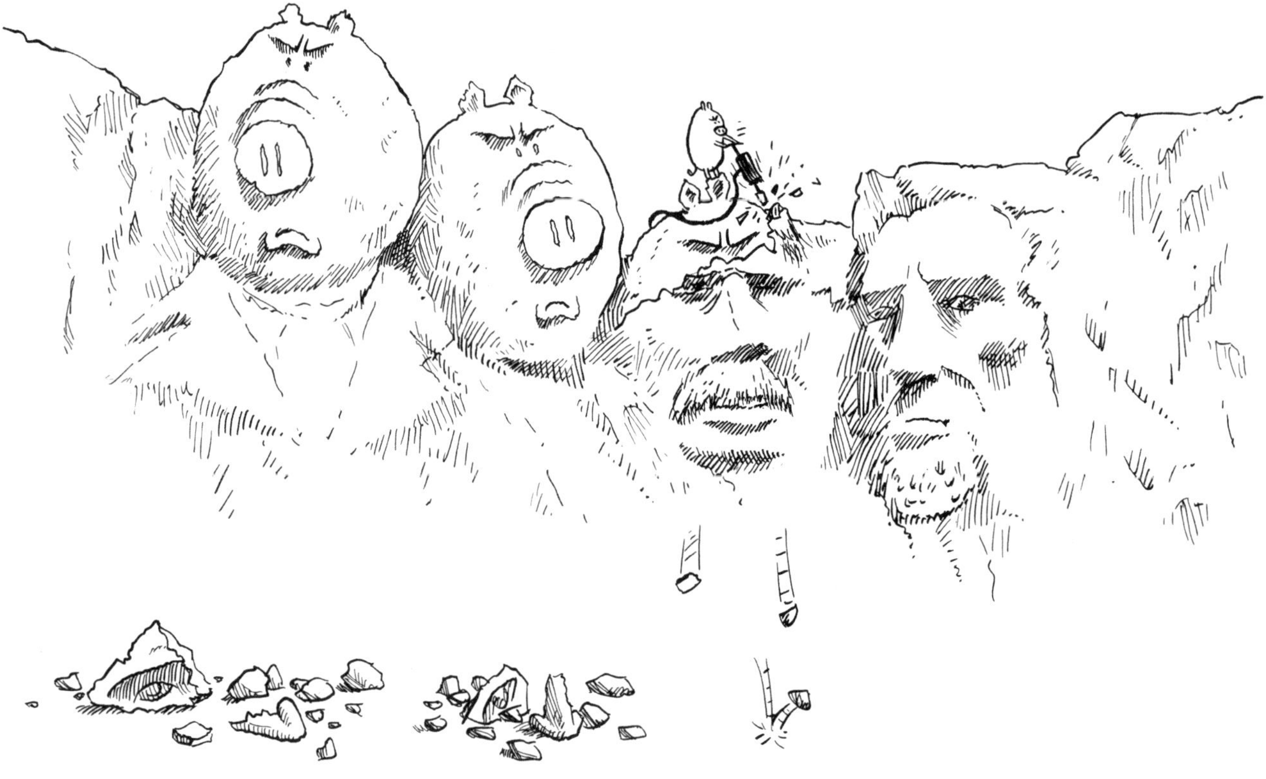

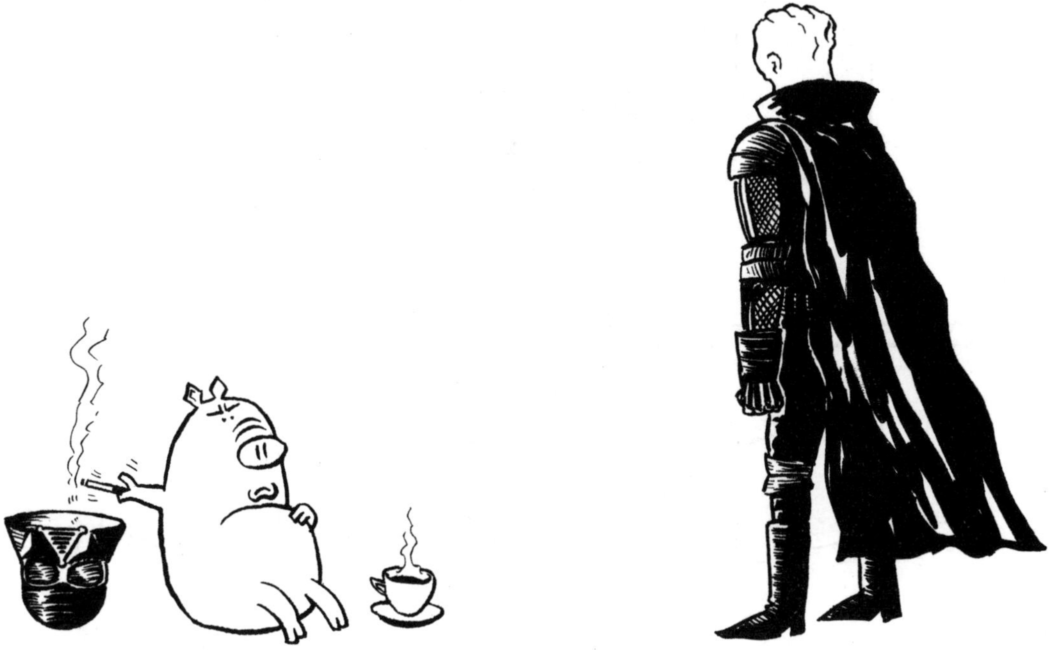

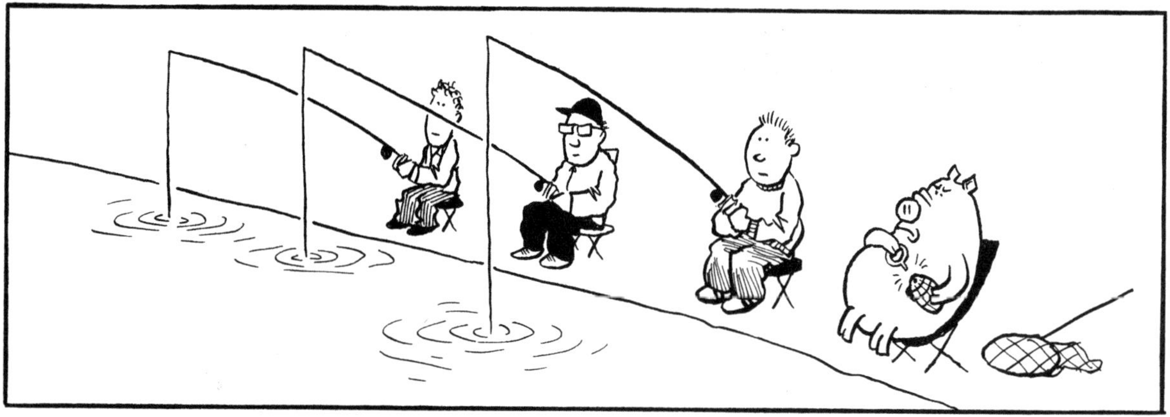

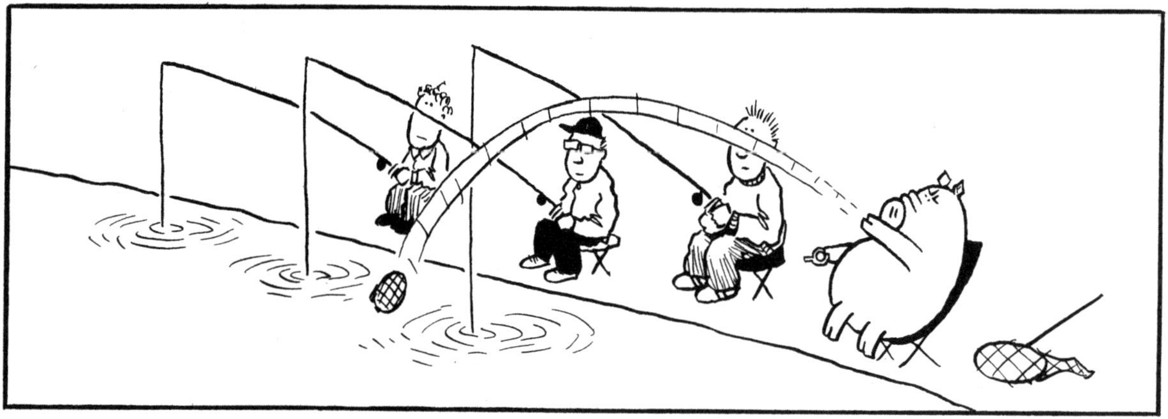

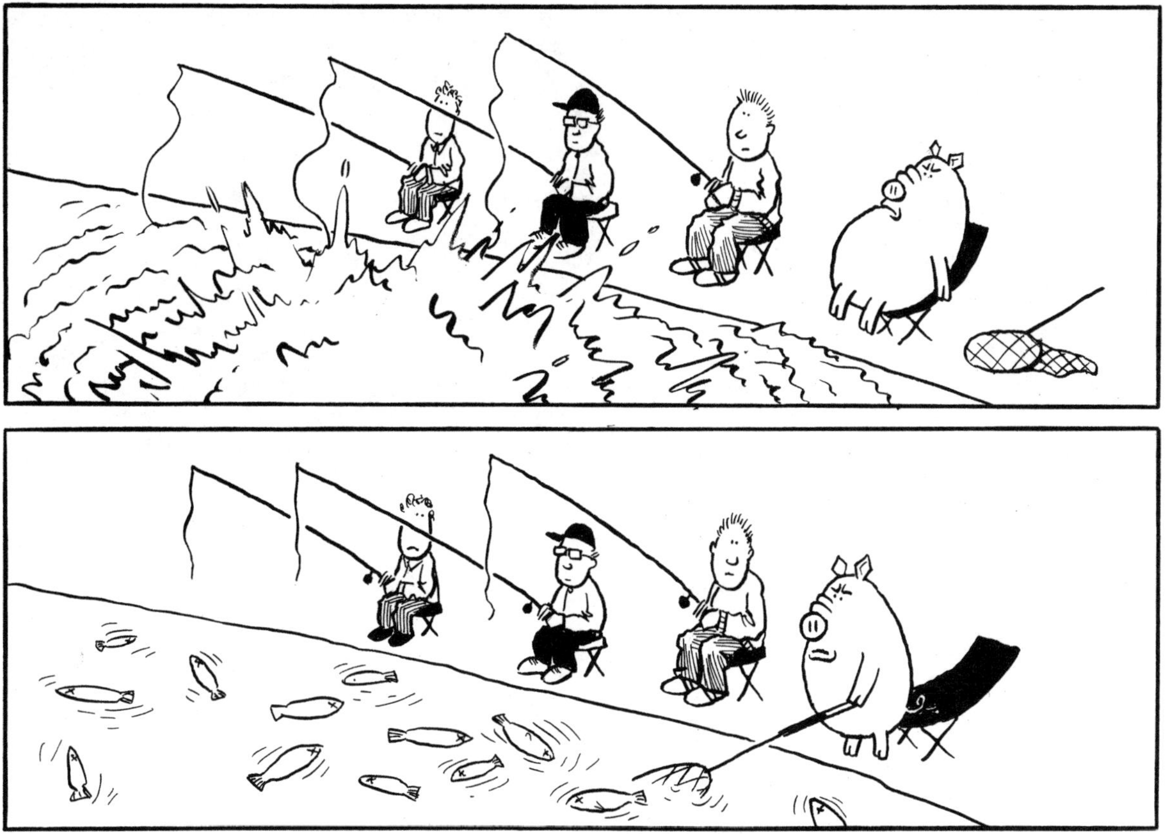

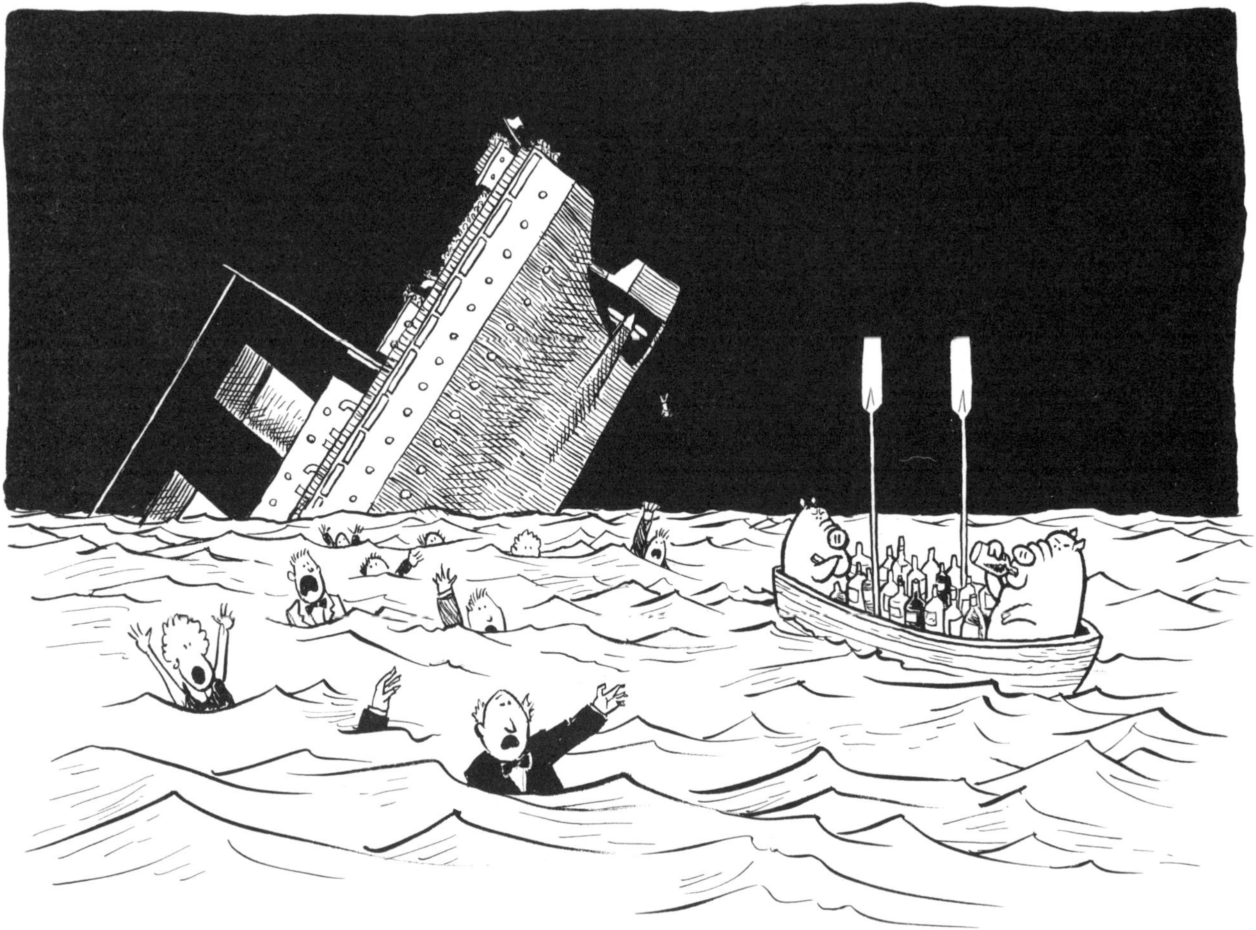

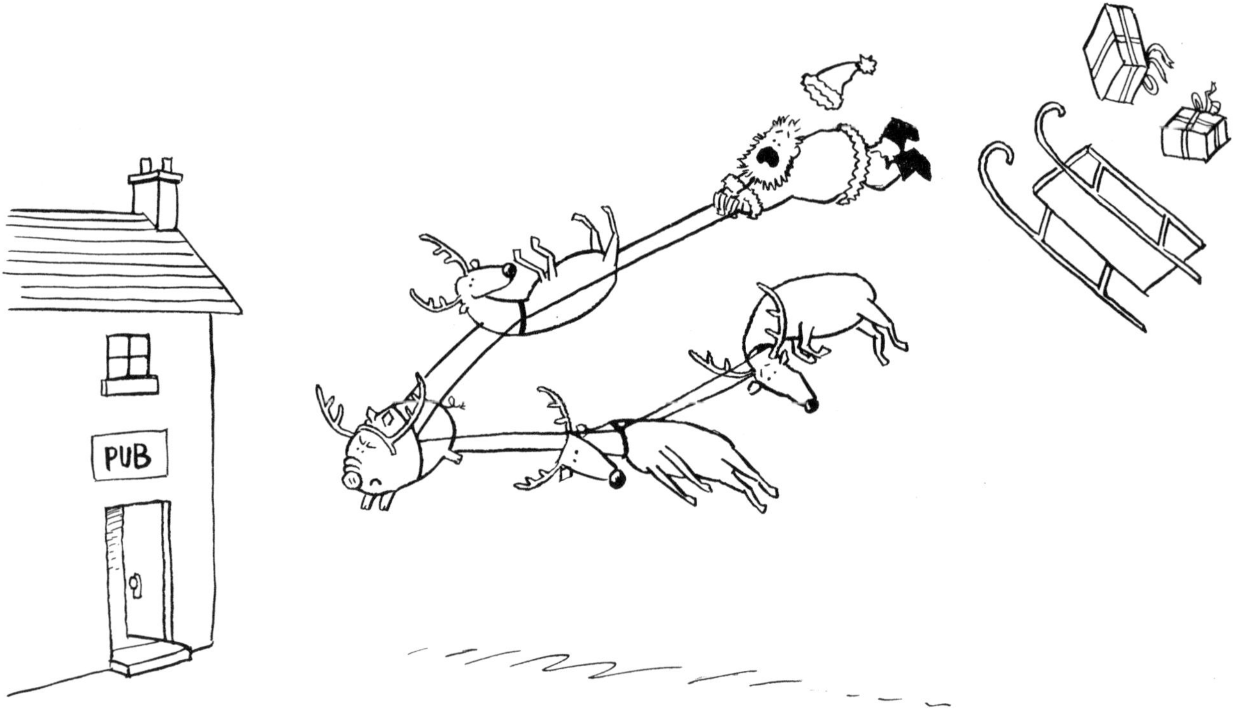
PUB

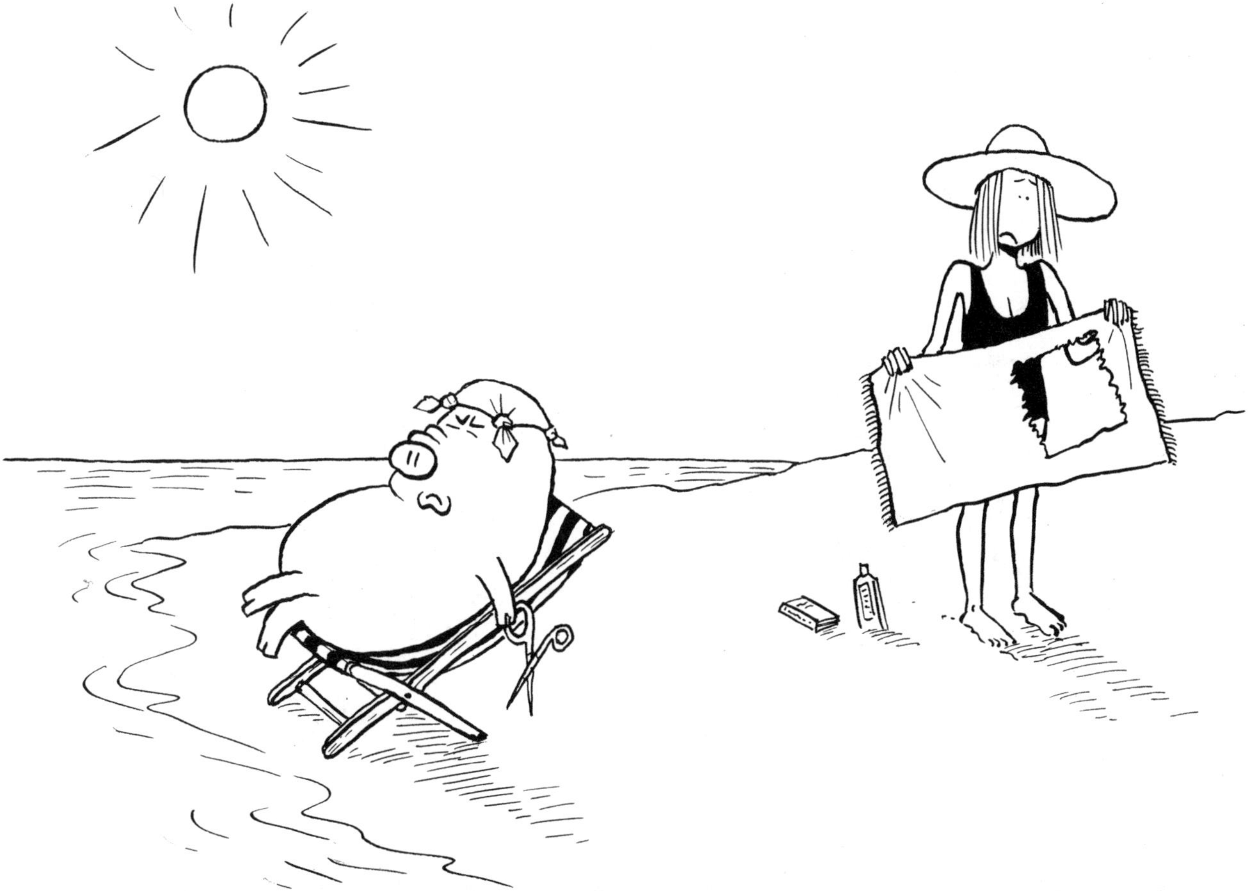

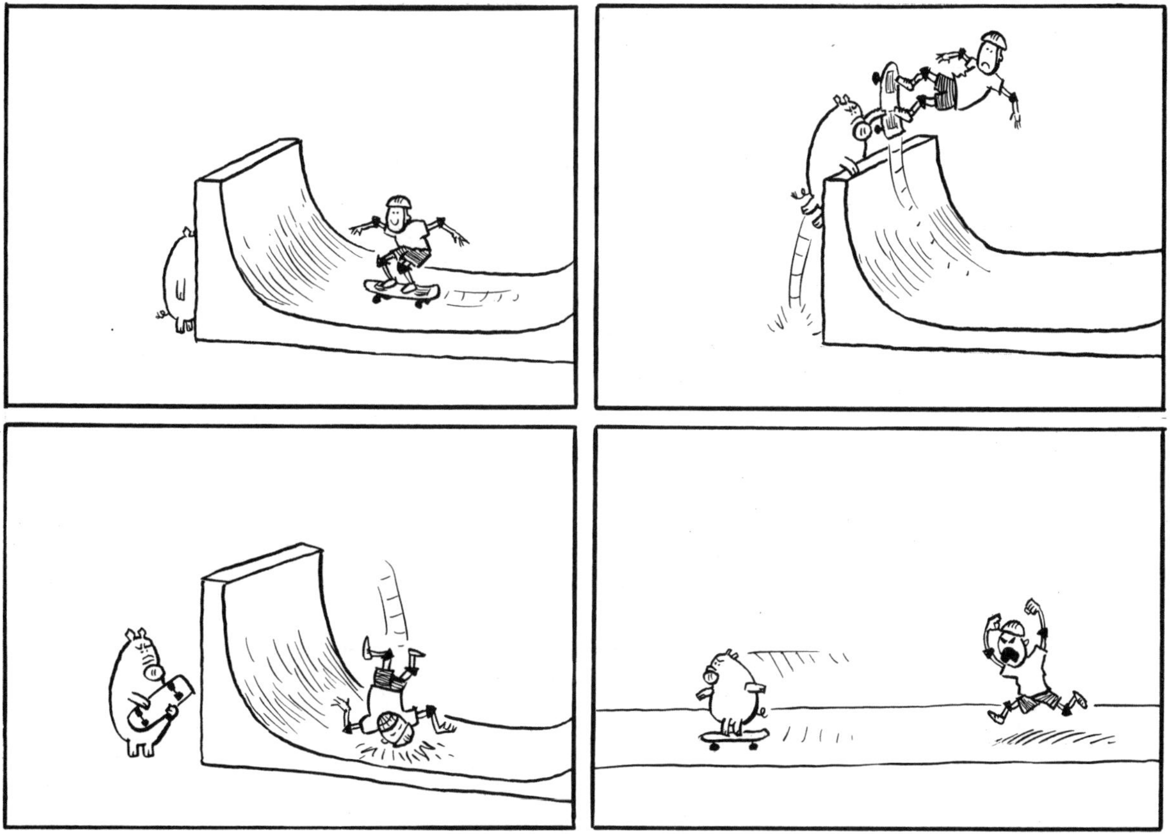

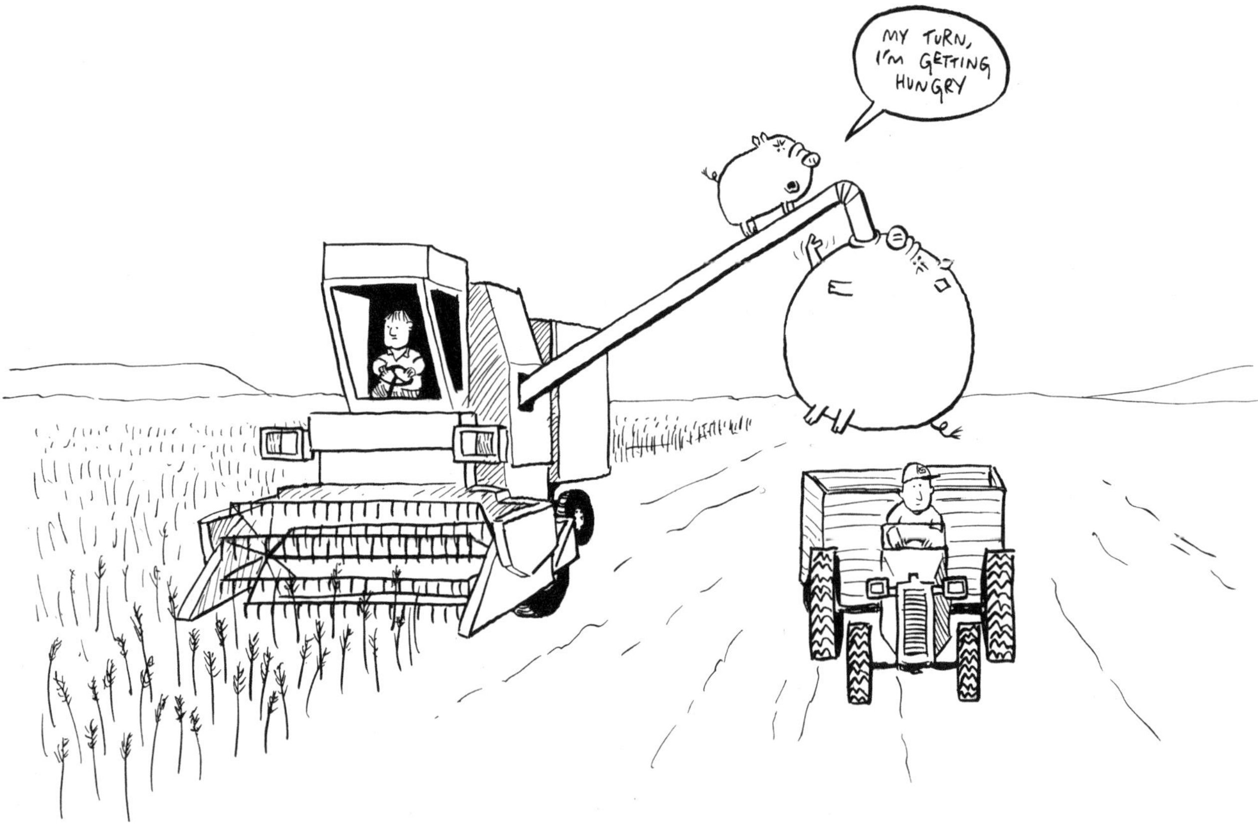
MY TURN, I'M GETTING HUNGRY

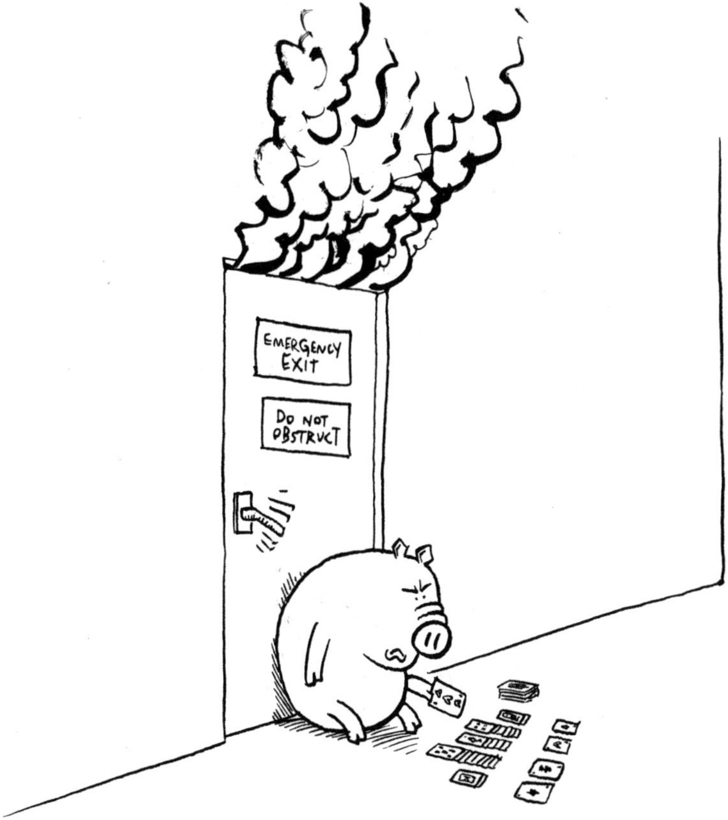
EMERGENCY EXIT
DO NOT OBSTRUCT

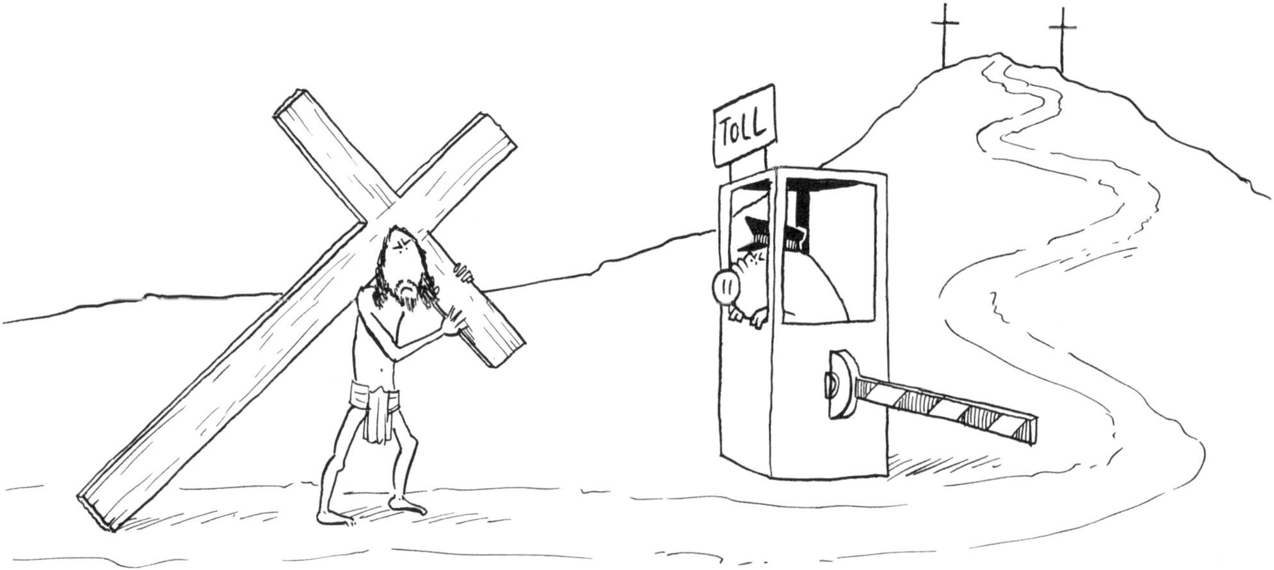
TOLL

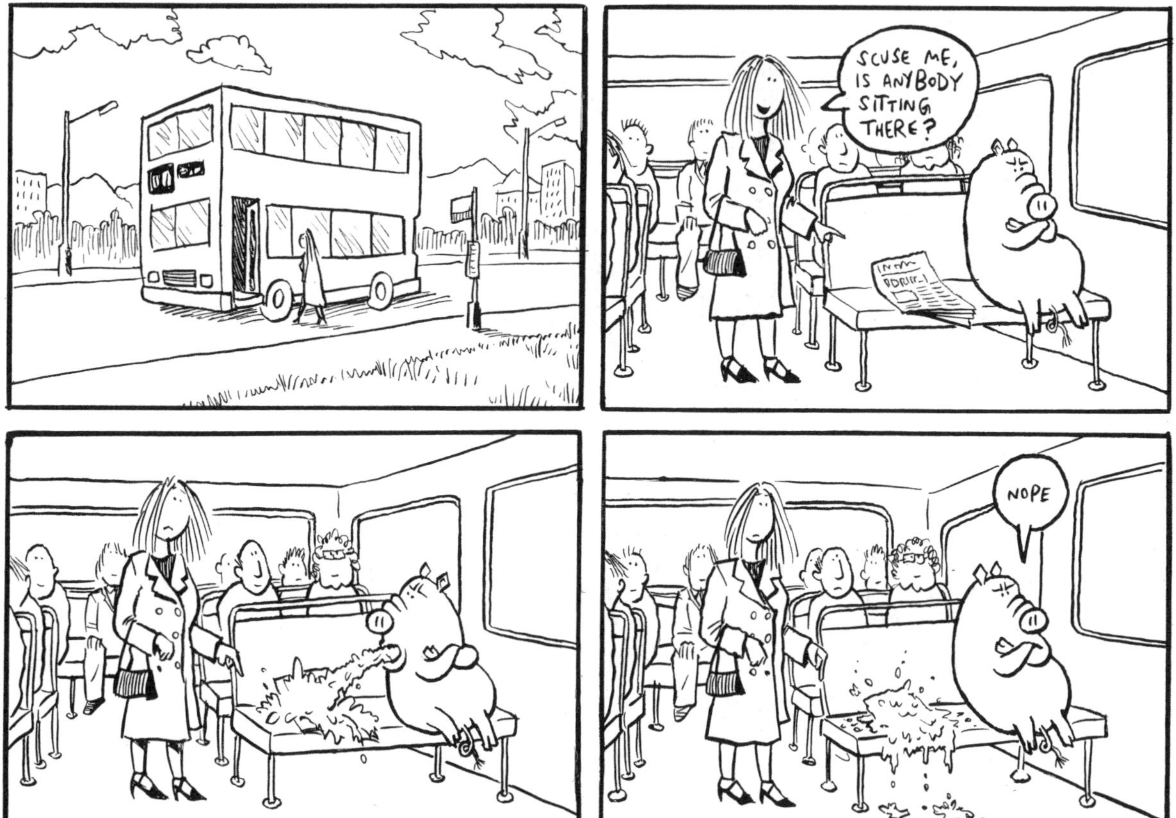
SCUSE ME, IS ANYBODY SITTING THERE?
NOPE

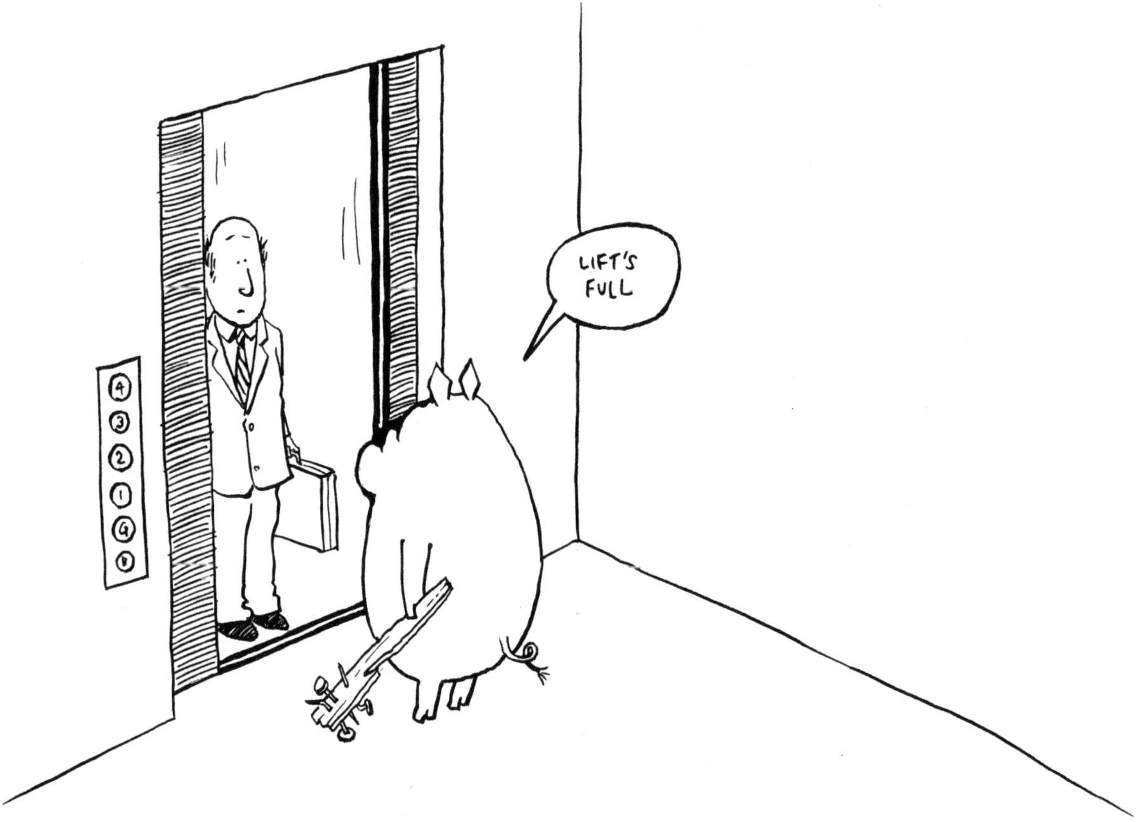
LIFT'S FULL

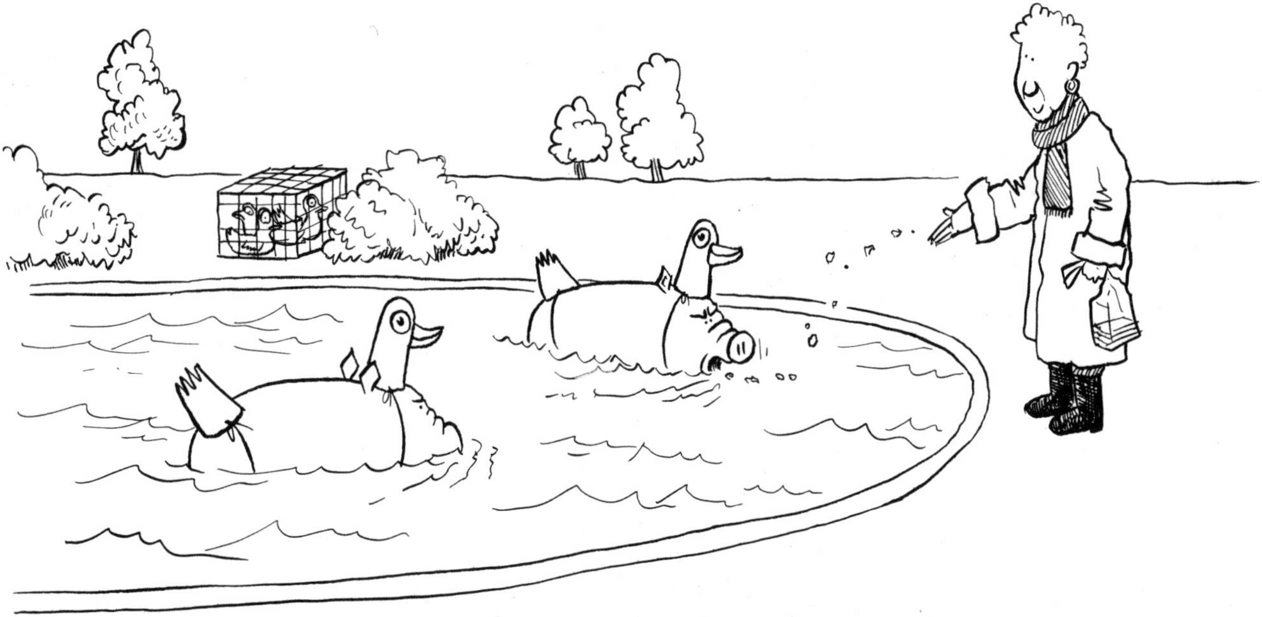

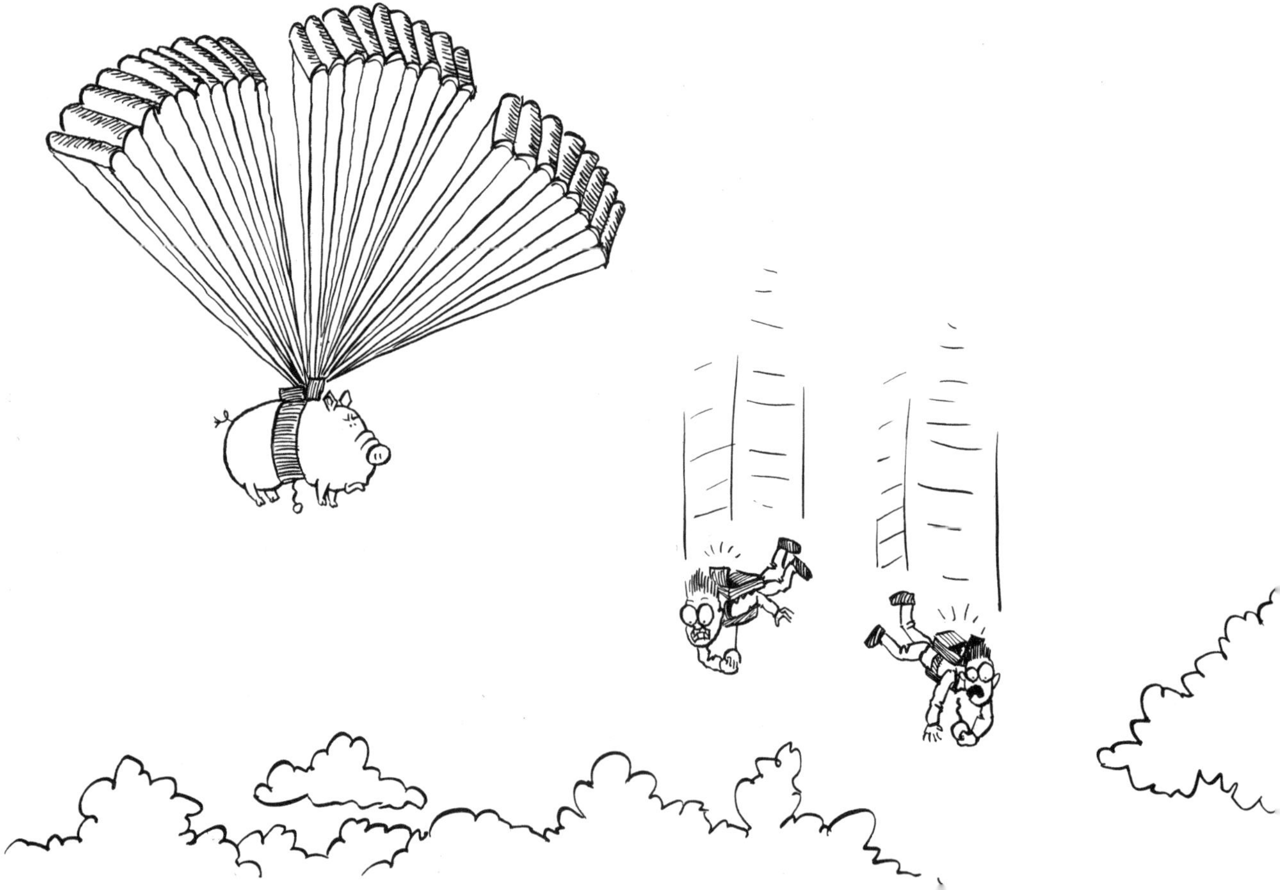

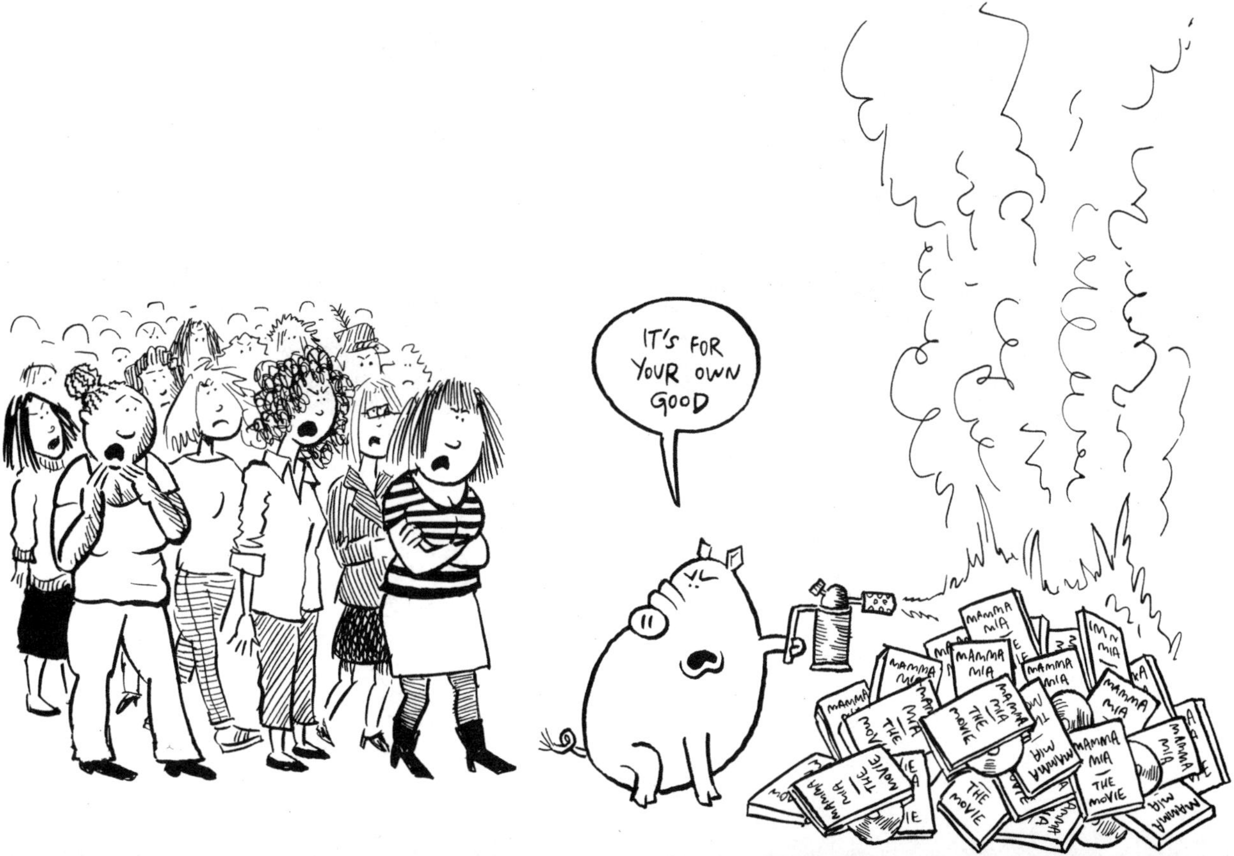
IT'S FOR YOUR OWN GOOD
MAMMA MIA — THE MOVIE

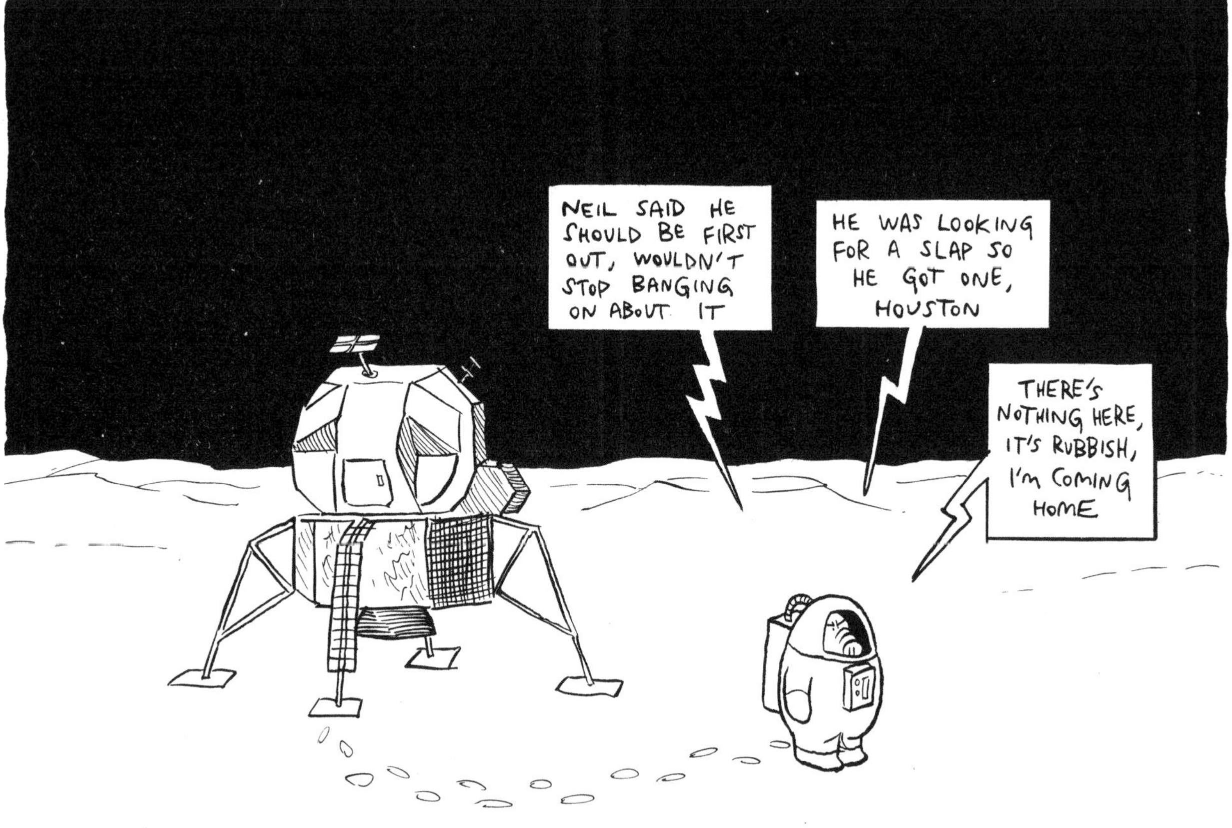
NEIL SAID HE SHOULD BE FIRST OUT, WOULDN'T STOP BANGING ON ABOUT IT
HE WAS LOOKING FOR A SLAP SO HE GOT ONE, HOUSTON
THERE'S NOTHING HERE, IT'S RUBBISH, I'M COMING HOME

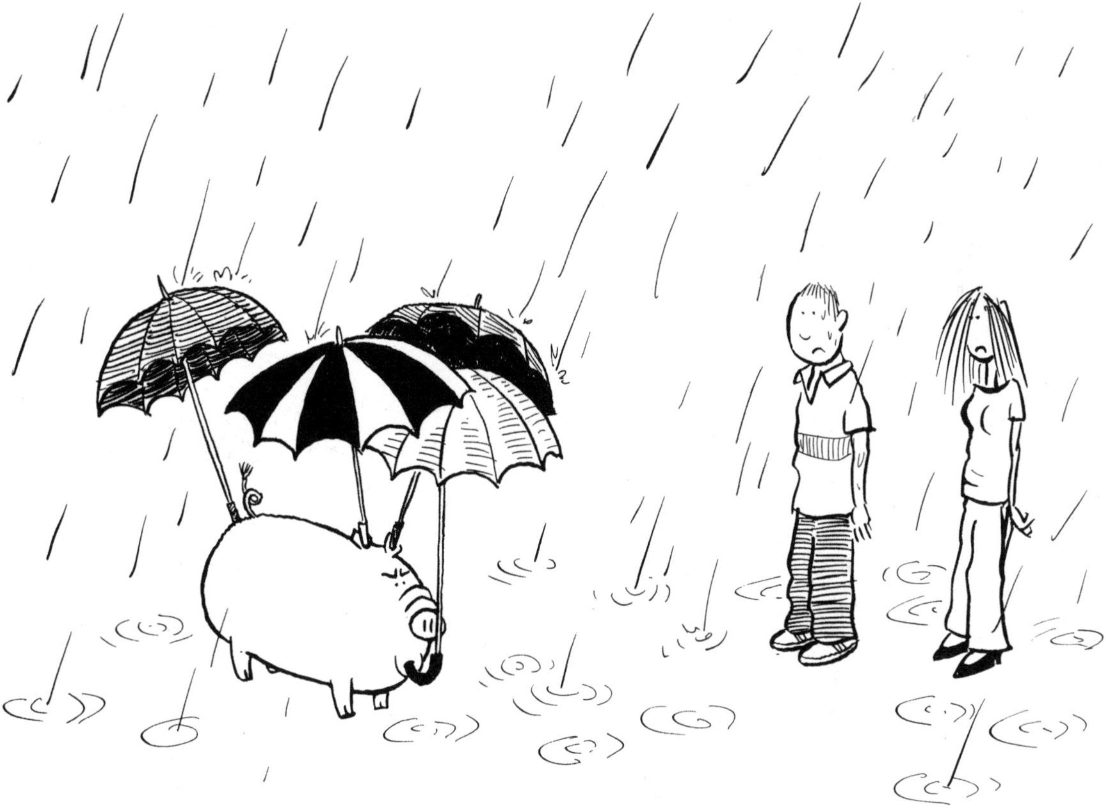

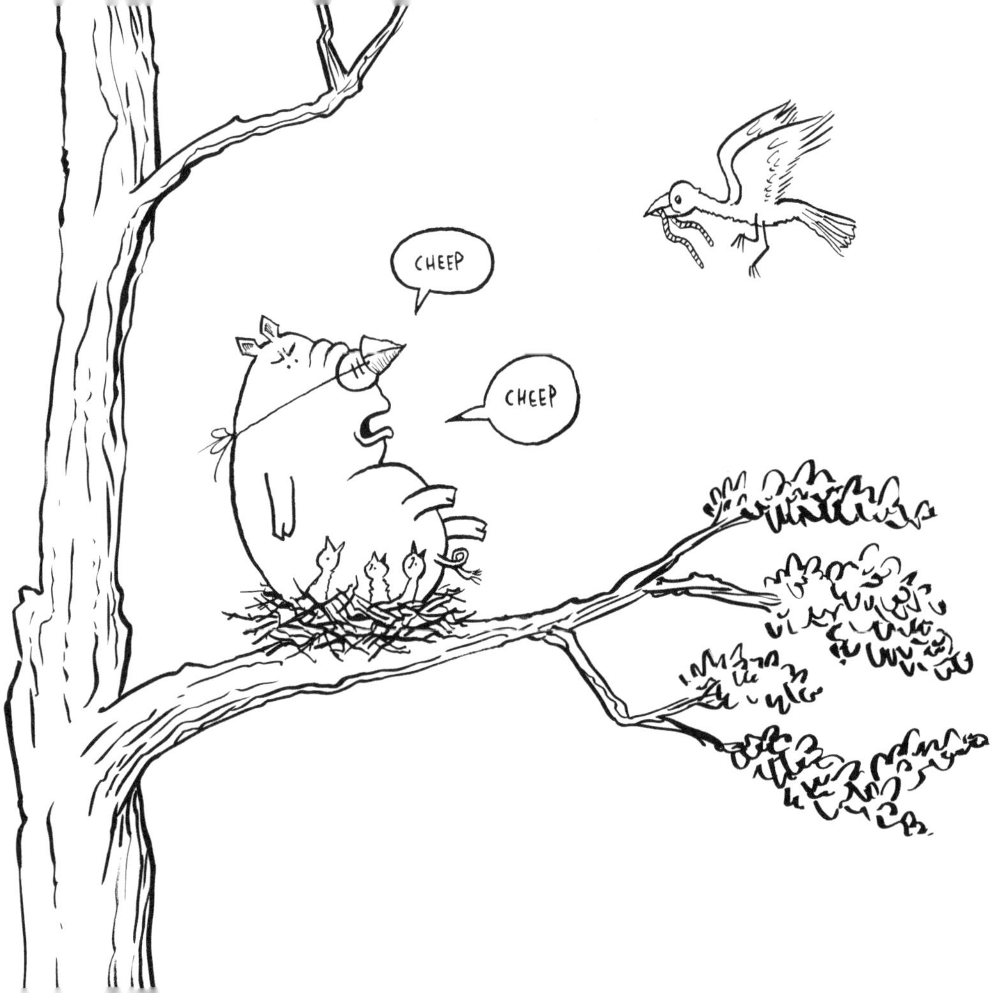
CHEEP
CHEEP

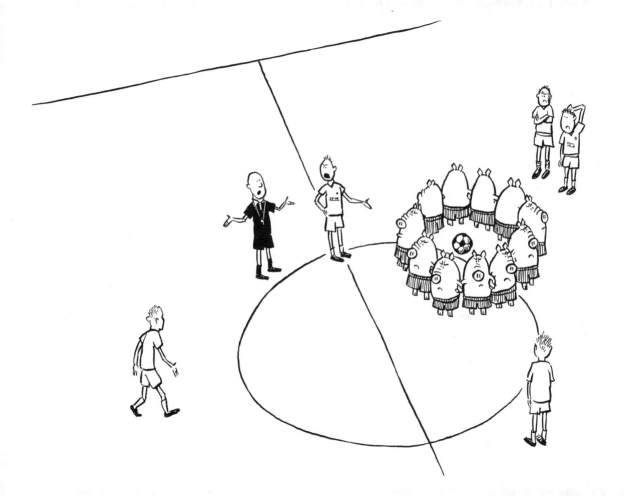

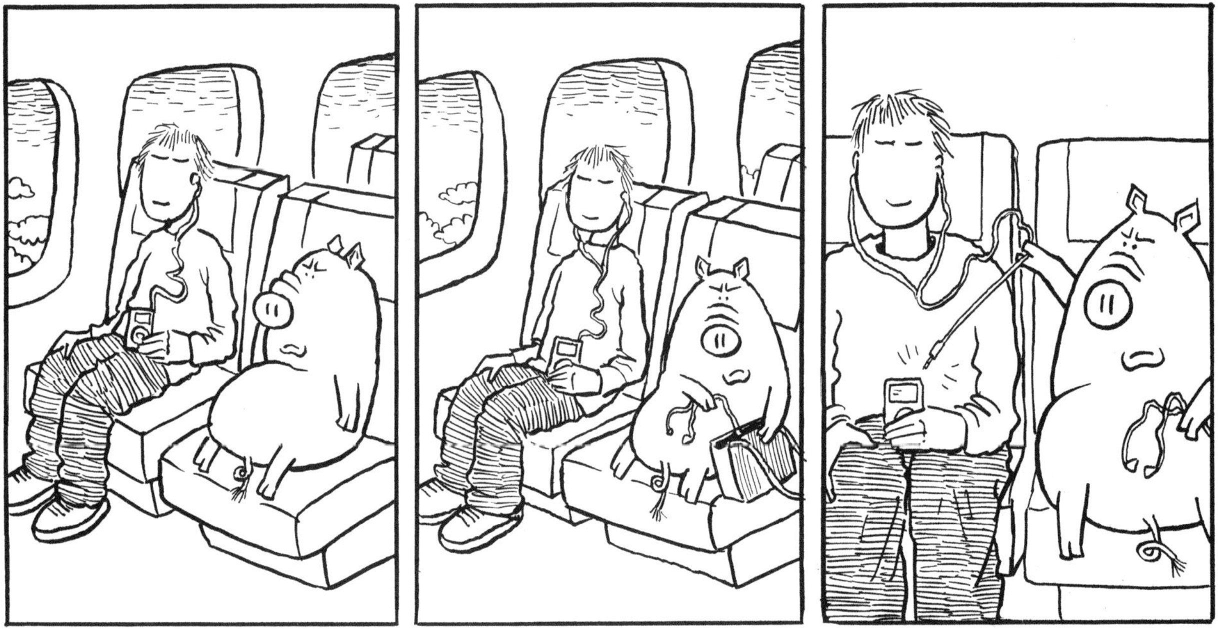

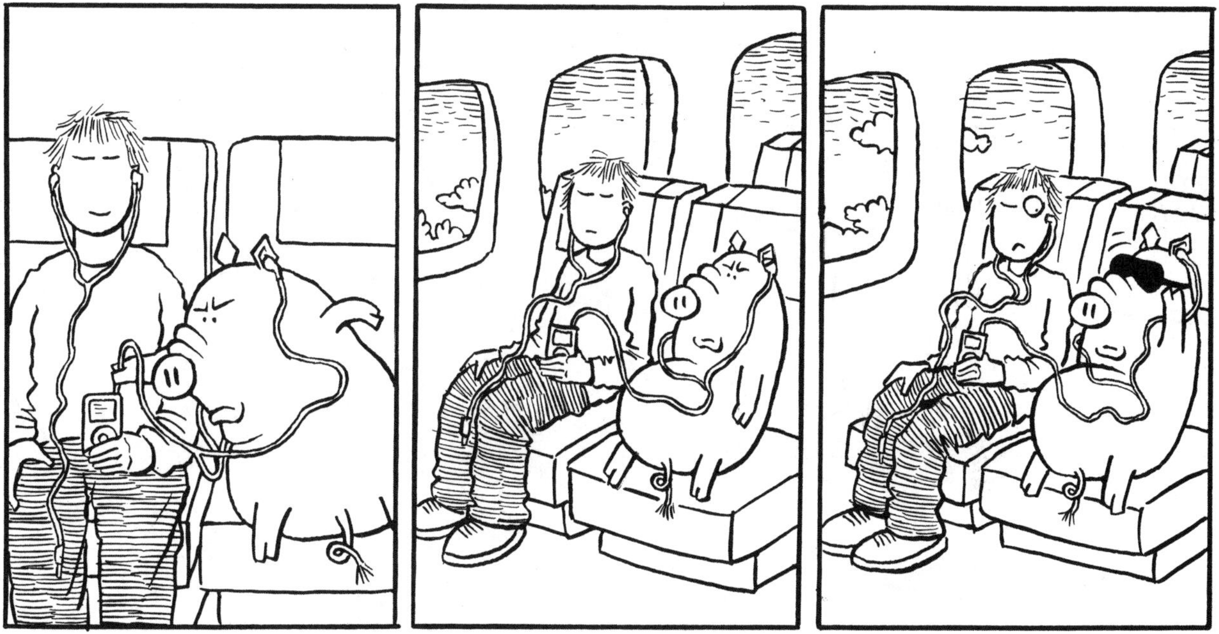

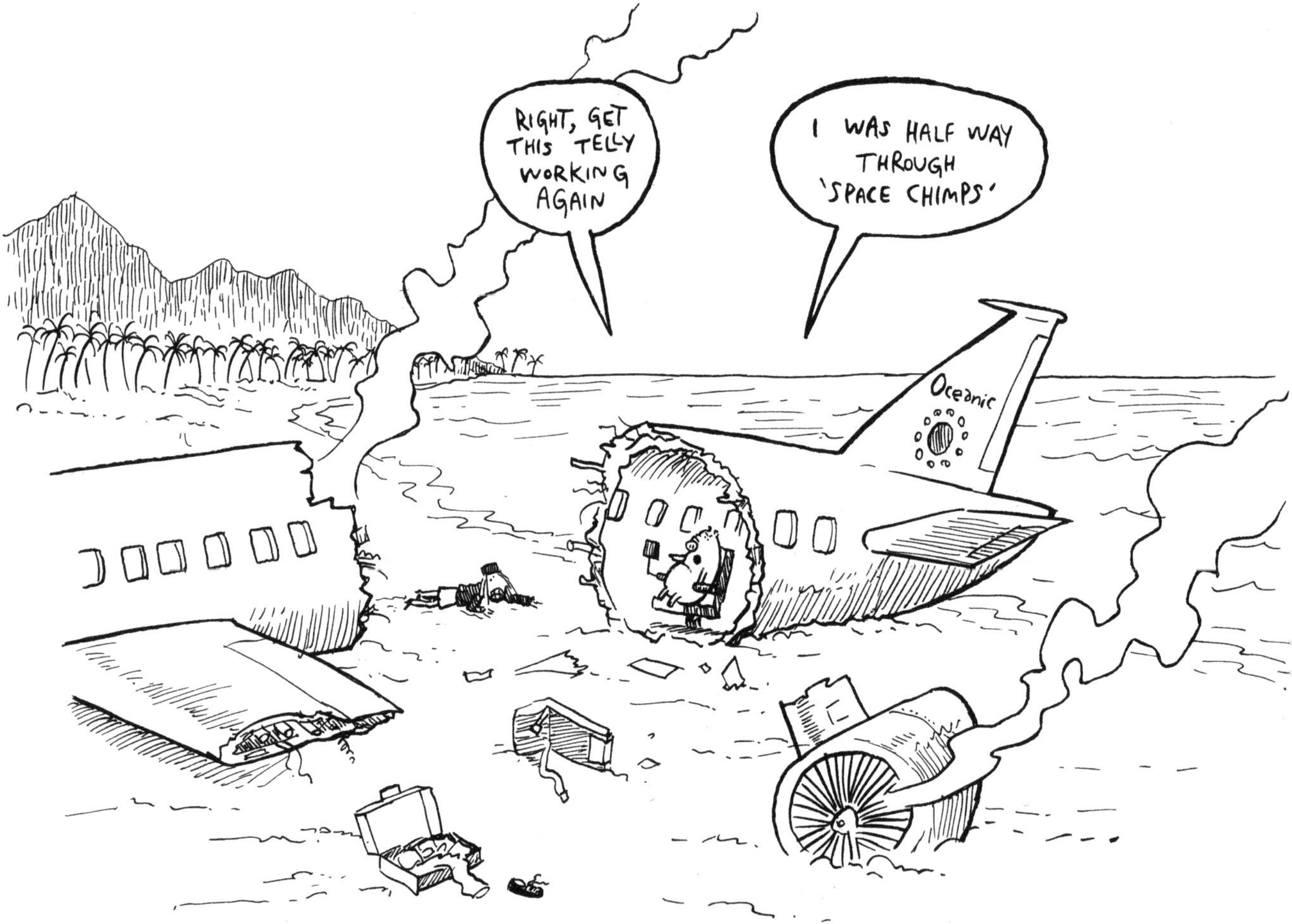
RIGHT, GET THIS TELLY WORKING AGAIN
I WAS HALF WAY THROUGH 'SPACE CHIMPS'
Oceanic

CAUSE YOU WERE BEING BORING

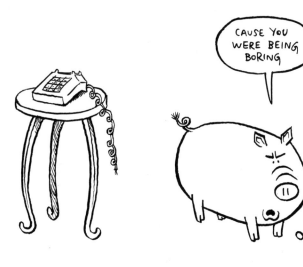

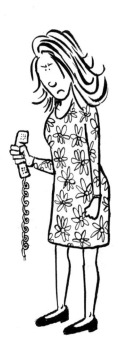

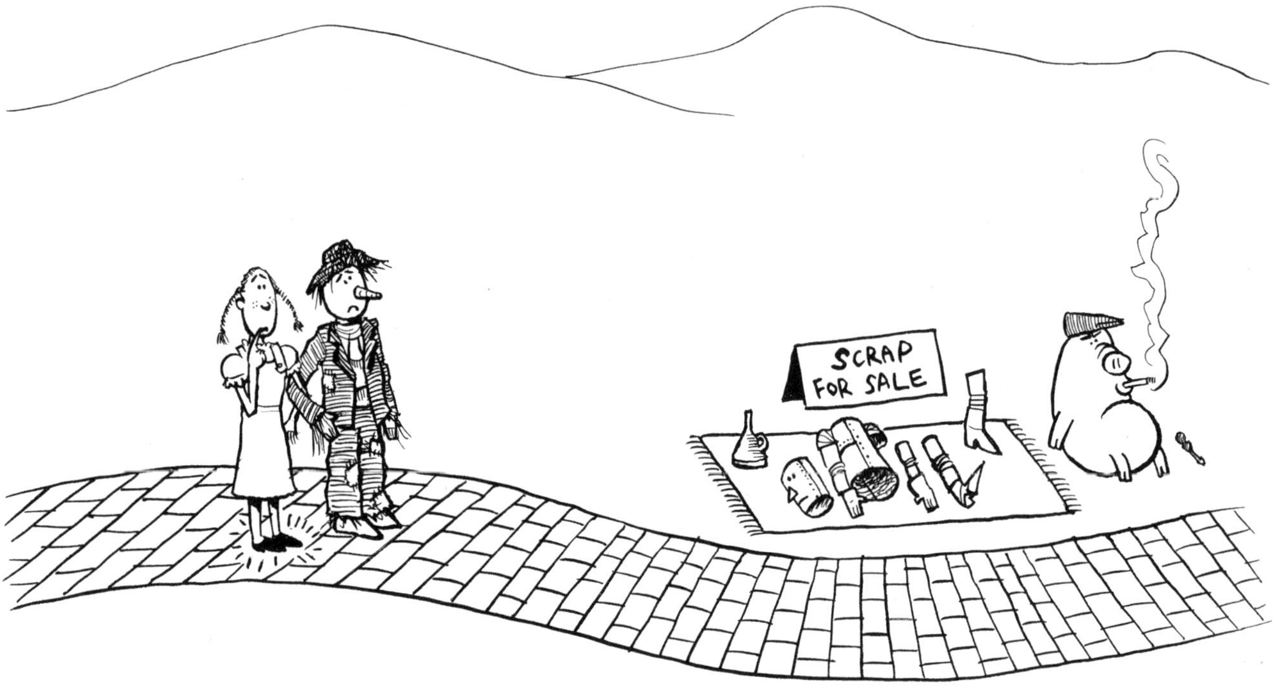
SCRAP
FOR SALE

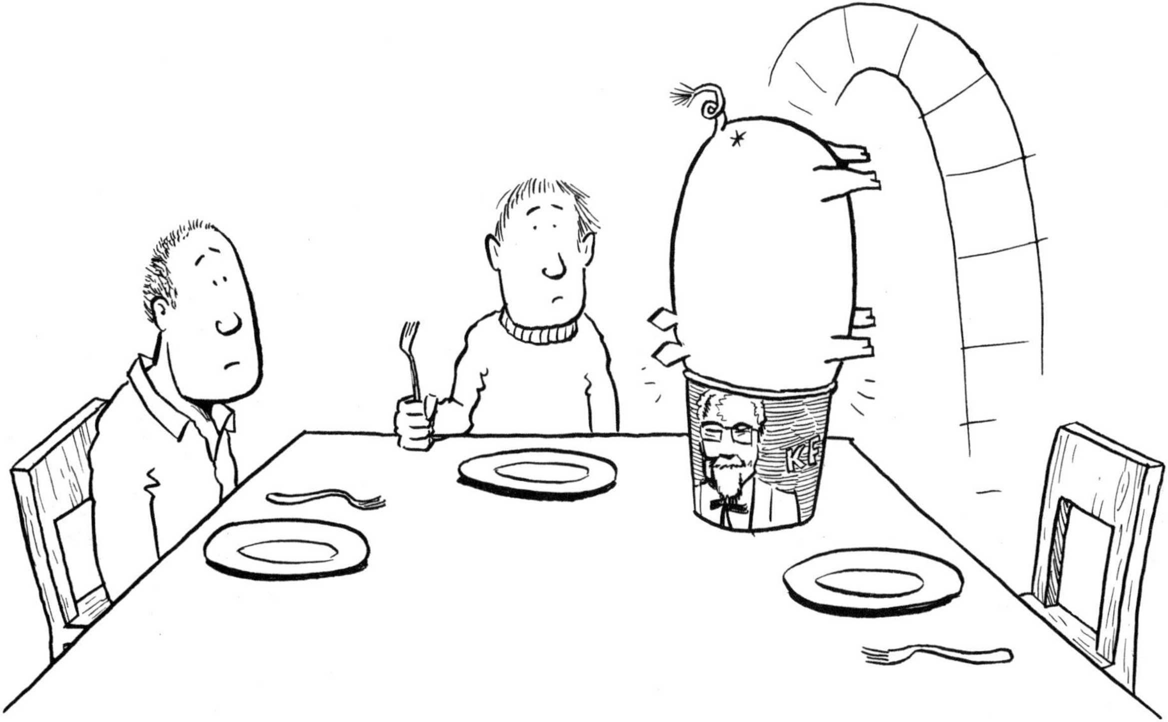
KF

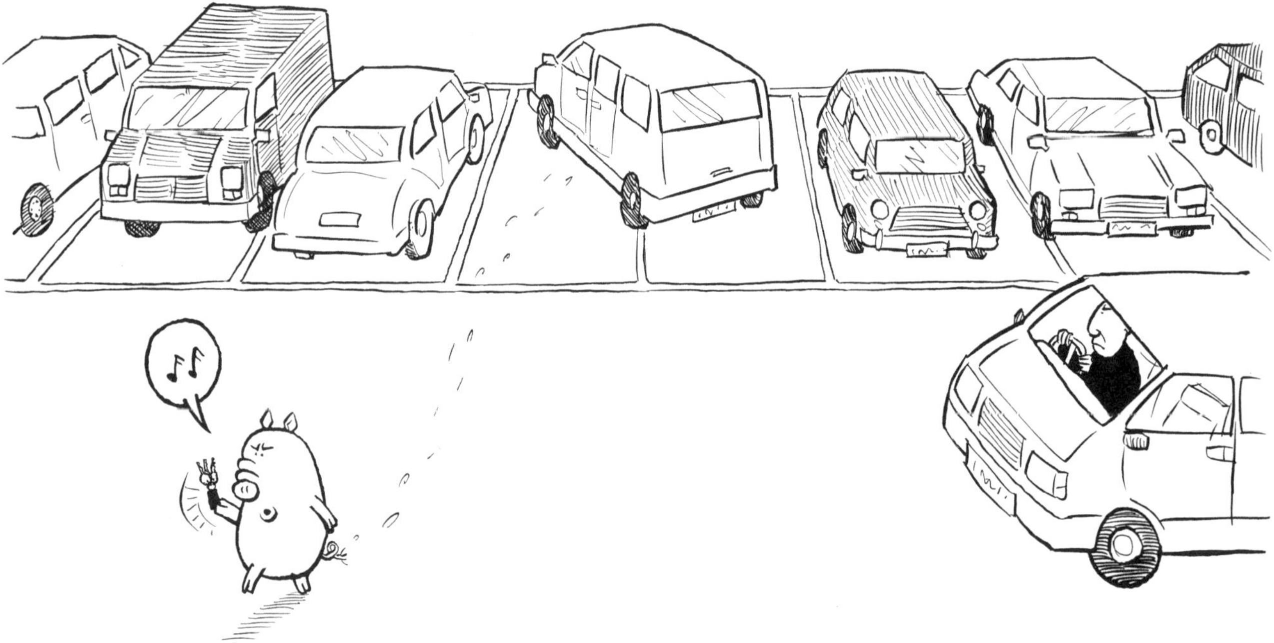

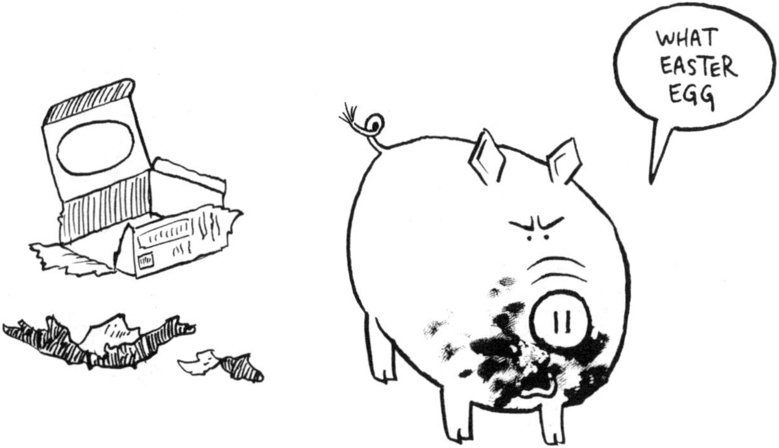
WHAT EASTER EGG

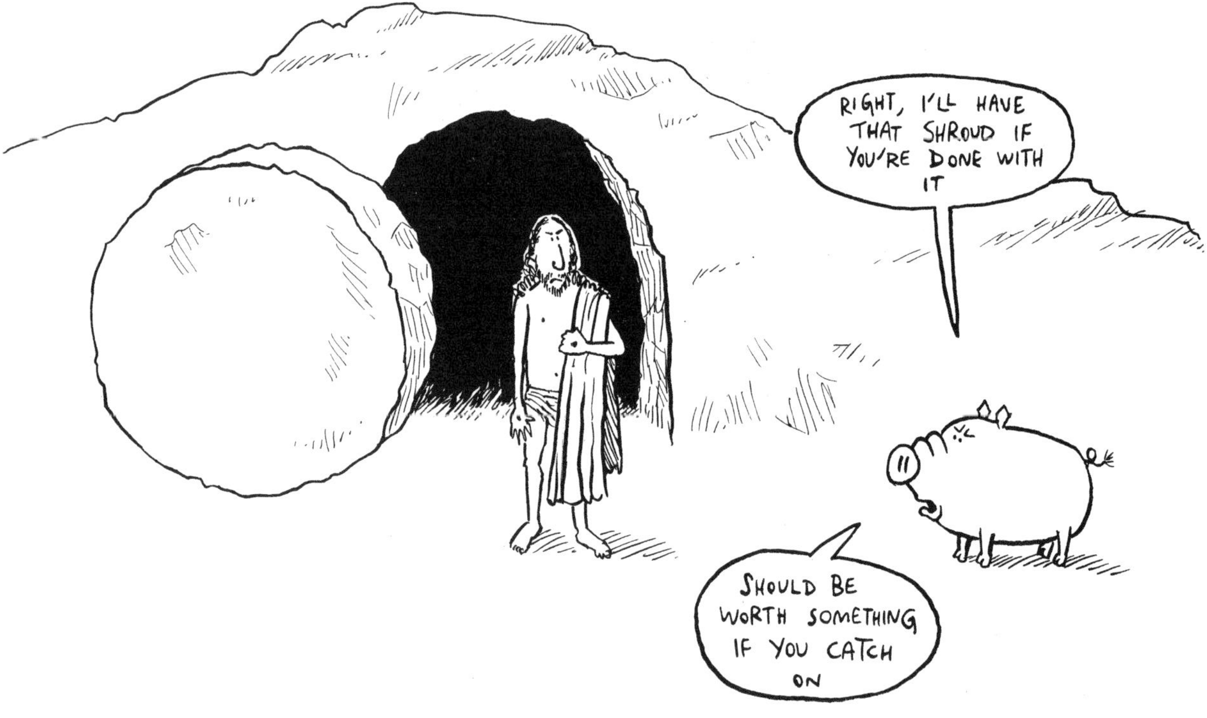
RIGHT, I'LL HAVE THAT SHROUD IF YOU'RE DONE WITH IT
SHOULD BE WORTH SOMETHING IF YOU CATCH ON

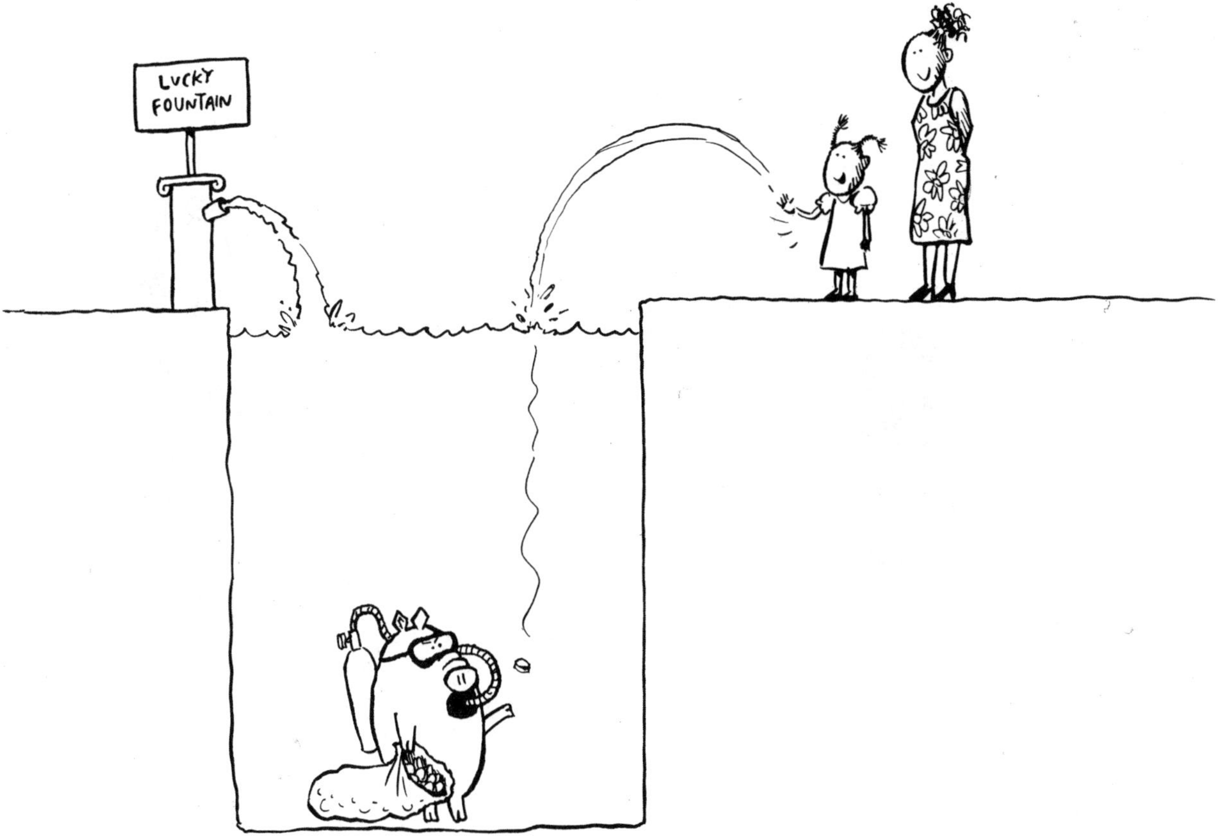
LUCKY
FOUNTAIN

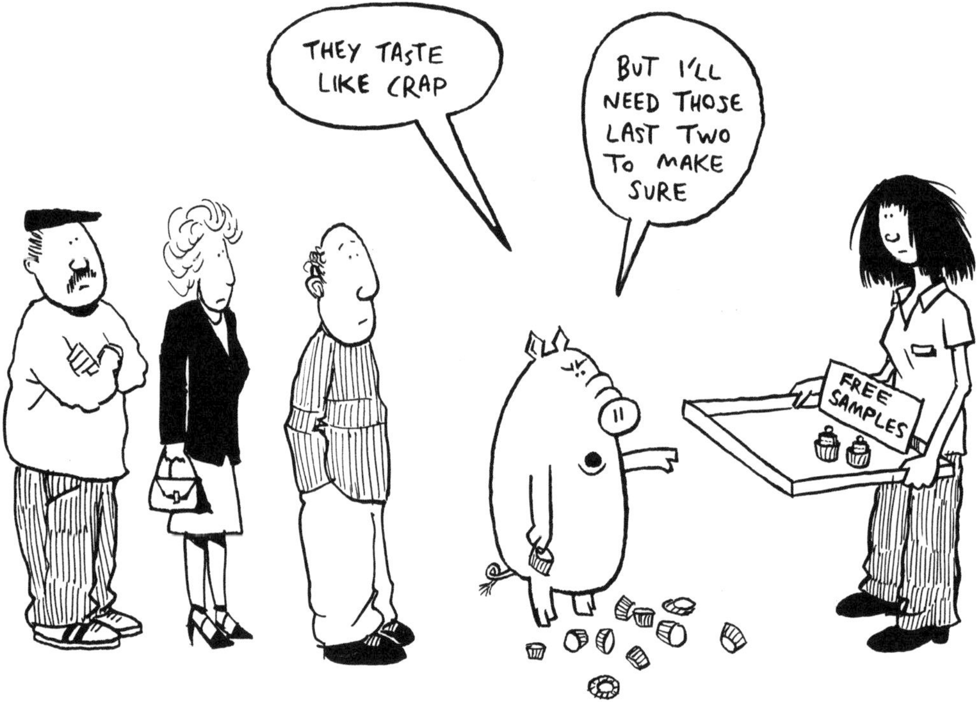
THEY TASTE LIKE CRAP
BUT I'LL NEED THOSE LAST TWO TO MAKE SURE
FREE SAMPLES

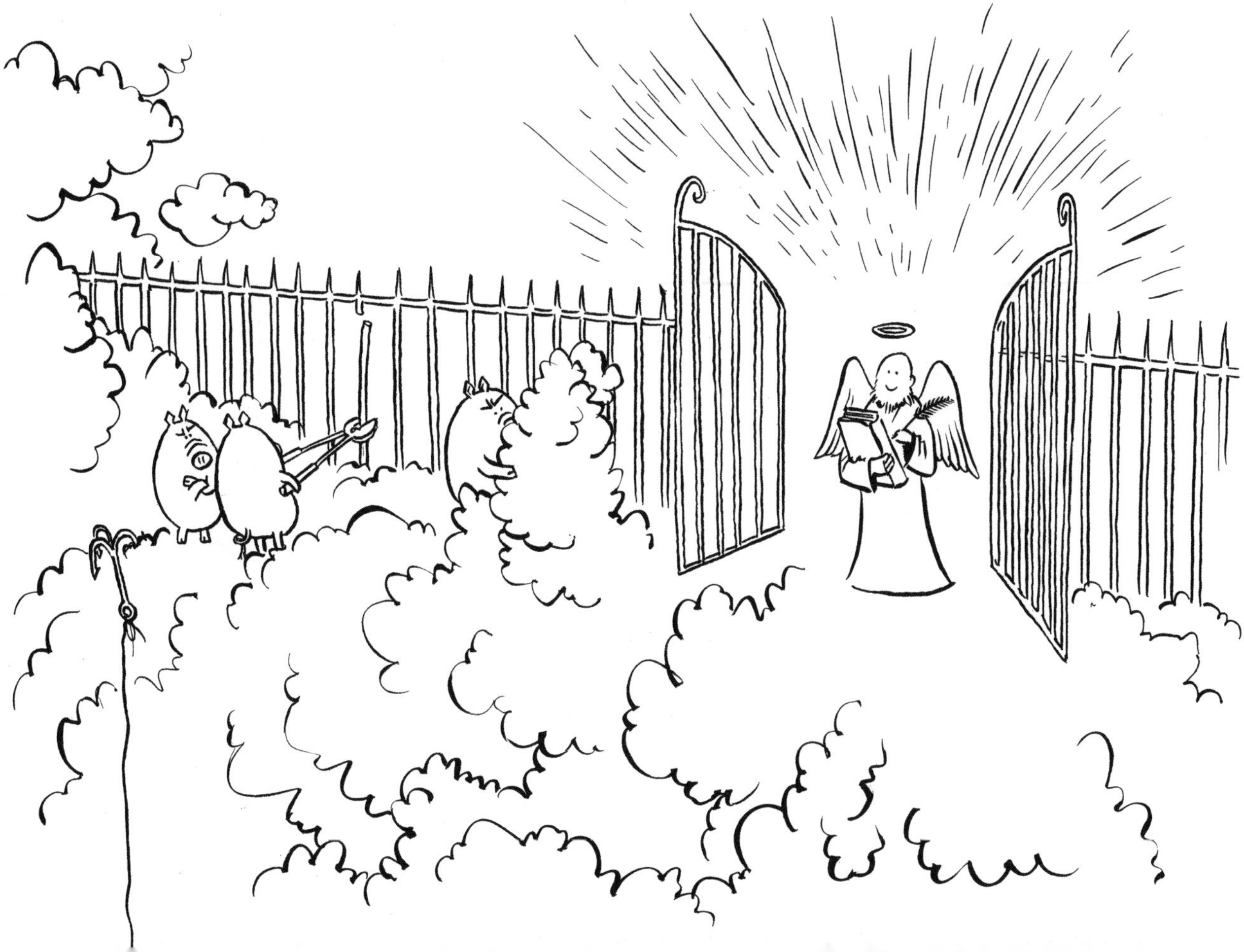

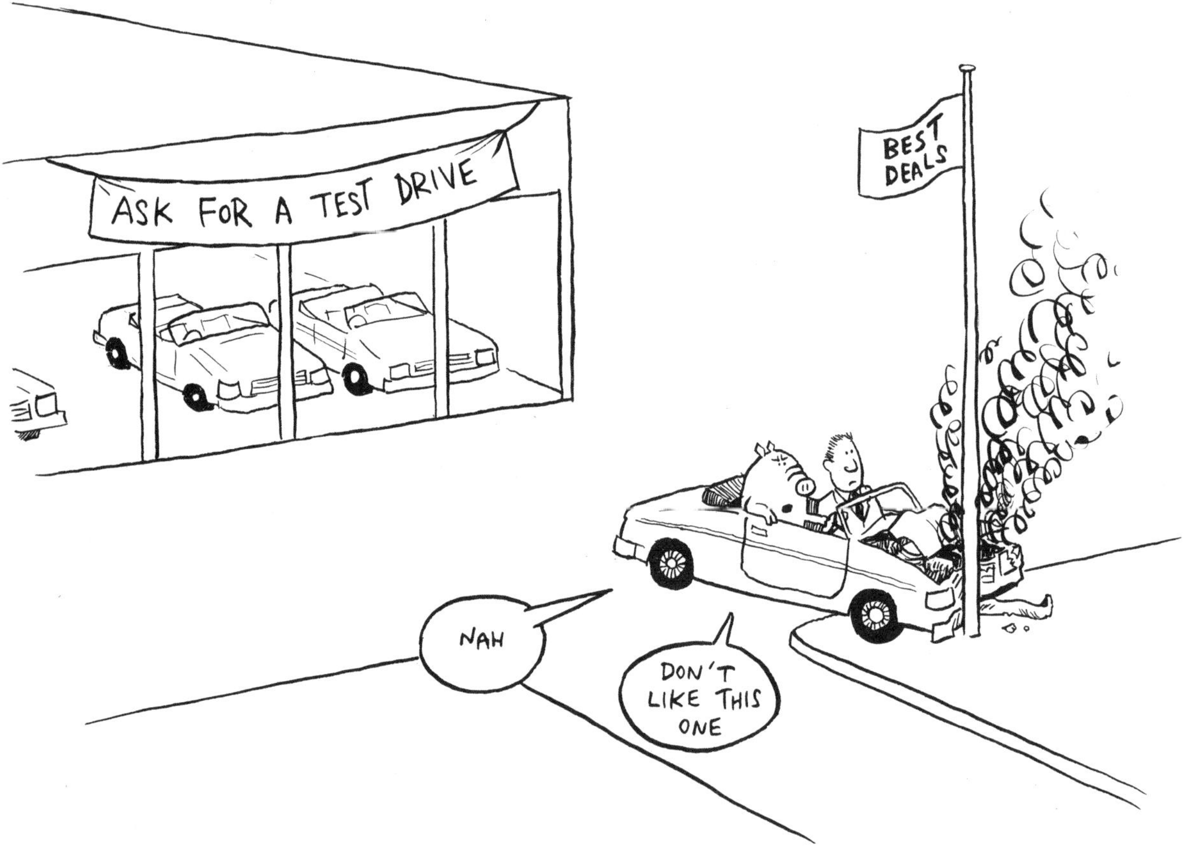
ASK FOR A TEST DRIVE
BEST DEALS
NAH
DON'T LIKE THIS ONE

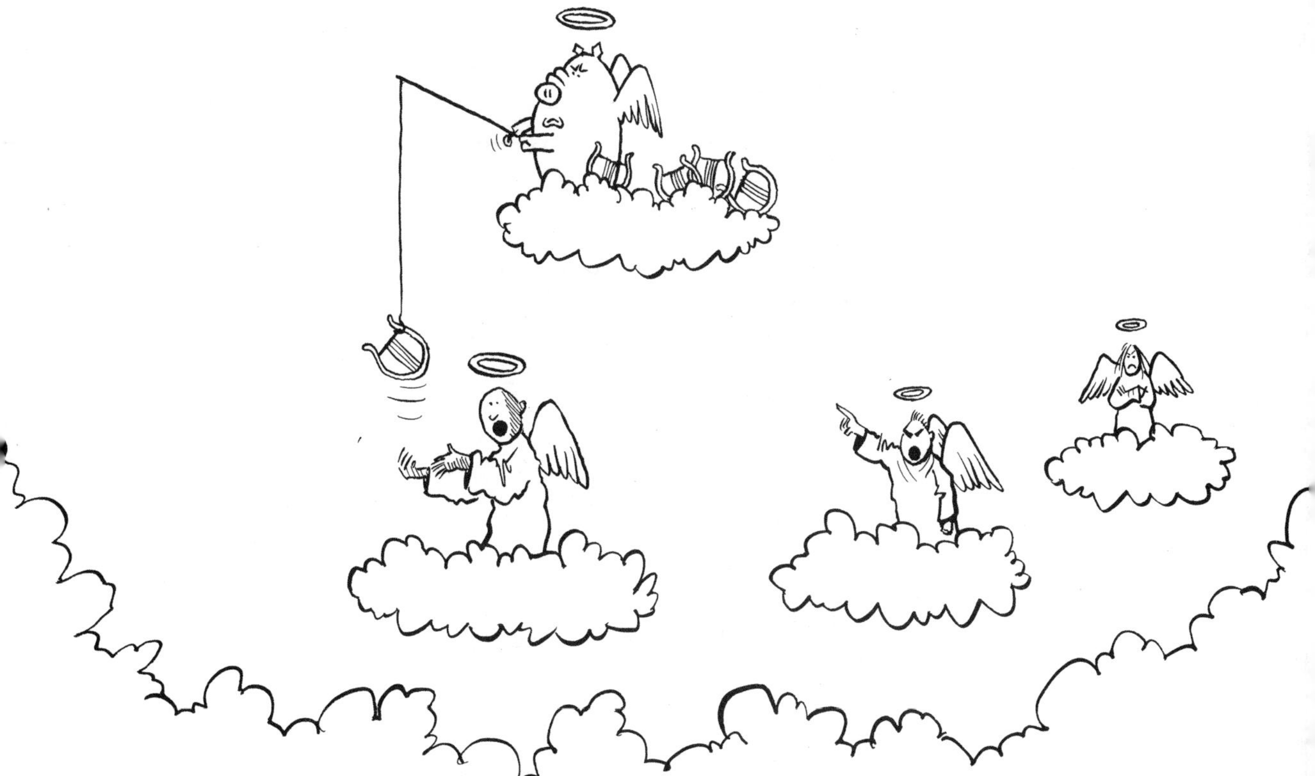

Andy Riley